W9-CJO-204

BIRDS

What's in a Name?

B I R

PETER BARRY

What's in a Name?

FROM *Accipiter* TO *Zoothera*

The Origin of Bird Names

First published in 2017 by Reed New Holland Publishers Pty Ltd
London • Sydney • Auckland

The Chandlery, 50 Westminster Bridge Road, London SE1 7QY, UK
1/66 Gibbes Street, Chatswood, NSW 2067, Australia
5/39 Woodside Avenue, Northcote, Auckland 0627, New Zealand

www.newhollandpublishers.com

A record of this book is held at the British Library and the National
Library of Australia.

ISBN 978 1 92554 604 0

Group Managing Director: Fiona Schultz
Publisher and Project Editor: Simon Papps
Designer: Andrew Davies
Production Director: James Mills-Hicks
Printer: Times Offset (M) Sdn Bhd, Malaysia

10 9 8 7 6 5 4 3 2 1

Keep up with New Holland Publishers on Facebook
www.facebook.com/NewHollandPublishers

Acknowledgements

My greatest thanks go to Dr Simon Papps, who led a group of birdwatchers to Iran in spring 2016, myself included, and trusted me enough to scribble a few pages on etymology.

I am extremely grateful to a little cohort of amateur artists, who have produced works of various kinds to illuminate the text, and include Jane Barry, Margaret Bradley, Catriona Hastings, Anita Inverarity, Doris Kanu, Kelechi Kanu, Maya Peter, Regina Sim and Erin Young. The youngest was aged eight years old, the oldest was the author.

My gratitude to Edgar Ferns, Donald Stuart, Gabor Czako and Peter Moran, who helped a non-techno birder to find his way through the mysteries of computer skills.

And thanks to those who spurred me on to the final lap, when I doubted the value of the text I had written.

In addition, thanks to the many birds, A to Z, who posed for me in my imagination.

Finally, thanks to those who have promised to buy a copy of the book, regardless of the quality. I will hold it to them, to aid the particular charity which will benefit from any proceeds: a truly memorable week in France, for children who have a variety of disabilities, and for the helpers who travel with them. This is a yearly event, in action for more than 60 years. In these simple ways, lives are transformed.

Image Credits

Jane Barry: pages 43, 56, 91r, 101b, 108b, 110, 123, 154b, 171.

Peter Barry: pages 7, 10, 23.

Margaret Bradley: page 108a.

Catriona Hastings: page 124.

Anita Inverarity: pages 26, 73, 89, 165.

Doris Kanu: page 166a.

Doris Kanu and Kelechi Kanu: pages 155. 162.

Kelechi Kanu: pages 24, 79, 87, 104, 135.

Maya Peter: page 64.

Shutterstock (individual photographer names in brackets): pages 11 (Georgios Kollidas); 5,12, 114, 139a, 168l (Morphart Creation); 13 (Marek Cech); 15a, 28 (Martin Prochazkacz); 15b (Noah Strycker); 19, 46, 137, 152 (Ondrej Prosicky); 20 (Gallinago_media); 22 (Sysasya Photography); 25, 70a, 71, 81, 96, 114, 119, 123, 125a, 197 (Dzmitry Yakubovich); 29, 97b (Tony Mills); 30 (Luca Nichetti); 31 (Karel Gallas); 35 (Vikpoint); 36 (22August); 37 (Mauricio S Ferreira); 39 (Elkin Restrepo); 41 (Chris Renshaw); 44–45 (Miao Liao); 47 (Bonnie Taylor Barry); 48 (FotoRequest); 49 (Sainam51); 51 (Chaminda Silva); 53 (John Carnemolla); 54, 168r–169 (Ivan Kuzmin); 55, 159a (Butterfly Hunter); 57 (Picattos); 58 (Miroslav Hlavko); 59, 66, 101a (Martin Pelanek); 60 (Everett Historical); 61, 172 (Brian Lasenby); 63 (Smishonja); 65 (Tomas Calle Boyero); 69 (Abi Warner); 70b (Houshmand Rabbani); 75 (Veselin Gramatikov); 76–77 (Sunsinger); 80 (Joe McDonald); 82 (Natalia Paklina); 83 (Colacat); 84 (Viktor Busel); 85, 131 (Steve Byland); 88 (Drakuliren); 90l (Clayton Burne); 90r–91l (Anton Ivanov); 93 (MCarter), 95a (Menno Schaefer); 97a (Uwe Bergwitz); 99 (Jesus Giraldo Gutierrez); 100, 124a, 136, 185 (Tim Zurowski); 102 (Josh Anon); 103 (Andriy Blokhin); 107 (Aaltair); 109 (Alfredo Maiquez); 111, 144 (Feathercollector); 113 (John L. Absher); 117 (Karel Bartik); 121 (Quincy Floyd); 122 (Dr Ajay Kumar Singh); 125b (Bearacreative); 127 (Tadas Jucys); 128 (Chris Watson); 129 (Carmine Arienzo); 133 (Donsimon); 135 (Dennis Jacobsen); 139b (Kent Ellington); 141 (Herman Veenendaal); 143 (Mark Medcalf); 145 (Rudmer Zwerver); 146 (Stanislav Beloglazov); 147 (Pino Magliani); 149 (Tone Trebar); 150 (Wolfgang Kruck); 157 (Sue Robinson); 158 (Hugh Lansdown); 159b, 163 (aDam Wildlife); 167 (Red Ivory); 175 (BMJ); 177 (SherSS); 178 (Soru Epotok); 179 (Hein Nouwens); 181 (Rich Carey); 182 (Dreamnikon); 184 (Giedriius); 186 (Chris Froome); 187 (Erni); 189 (Marc Turcan); 191 (Super Prin); 193 (Radovan Zierik); 195 (DayuYu); 199 (Mircea C); 200 (Narupon Nimpaiboon).

Regina Sim: pages 95b, 151, 154a, 166b, 190.

Erin Young: page 27.

CONTENTS

Binomials: an Introduction

Aristotle and Plato

The School of Athens, a painting by
Raphael, shows Aristotle and Plato in
debate. The subject is 'reality'. Where is it
to be found? Plato points upwards to the
world of the unseen and metaphysical.
Aristotle points downwards and
finds reality at his feet and the world
around him. For Aristotle the study of
living organisms will proceed through
observation. Aristotle was one of the
first scientists to organise living things
into groups and categories – a science
called taxonomy. We might (humorously,
of course) use some of the vocabulary
favoured by birdwatchers today. If Plato
favours the 'armchair tick', then Aristotle
is 'the finder in the field'!

Plato and Aristotle in *The School of Athens*.

For Aristotle (384–322 BC),
empiricism, understanding nature through
simple observation, was the way forward.
This worldview is shown in his seven-
volume book on the natural world, which was remarkable for its time. This huge tome
set the groundwork for any future work on taxonomy, or how species can be better
understood when grouped together by their similarities and differences.

Aristotle finished the work in 350 BC, by which time he had begun to tutor
Alexander the Great. This was the most comprehensive study of living organisms for
its time.

Many of the names used by Aristotle have endured until today. *Perdix* is the name
for the partridge, *corax* for the raven, *phalacrocorax* for the cormorant, and *epops* for
the hoopoe.

The principles laid down by Aristotle survived for almost 2,000 years.

Aristotle, of course, made many 'schoolboy howlers'. He thought that birds which were promiscuous lived shorter lives, that they were corrupted by too much sex. Intemperate lust was thought to enfeeble the body.

Again, no-one had any idea why some species of birds, for example swallows, disappeared during the winter and reappeared in the summer. Aristotle thought swallows gathered in flocks in the autumn, and plummeted collectively into riverbeds until the warmth of the spring sun awoke them. Whatever his shortcomings here, his work on the

The father of modern taxonomy, Carl Linnaeus.

classification of living organisms provided a sound basis for the much-later binomial classification of Linnaeus. For example, Aristotle defined a human being as '*zoon politicon*': humans belonged to a grouping of living things (zoon, or animal), and differed from other living things by their ability to do politics.

'Man', for Thomas Aquinas (1225–1274) and other schoolmen, was a 'thinking animal'.

The binomial system of Carl Linnaeus (1707–1778) was already anticipated by the medieval philosophers, who defined 'Man' as 'animal rationale'. *Animal* was considered a genus, and *rationale* was a characteristic, what we might call today the 'specific difference'. Carl Linnaeus is known by the epithet, the 'father of modern taxonomy'.

Linnaeus, who lived in the 18th century, used Aristotle's classifications in his own work. His book, *Systema Naturae* began as a work of 15 pages. By the ninth edition Linnaeus had classified 4,400 species of birds and animals and 7,700 species of plants.

Various unwieldy names and untidy categories became systemised through his use of binomials. Thus the Common Chaffinch was a finch whose genus was expressed by the word *Fringilla*, but it differed from other family members in colour and habit. This difference was expressed in the word *coelebs*. The specific word means 'celibate', as Linnaeus noticed that the male and female chaffinches separated in the winter. Put simply, the bird was *Fringilla coelebs* (literally translated as 'the celibate finch').

In the same way, the Herring Gull belonged to the genus *Thalassa*, a Greek word which meant 'of the sea', and differed from other members of the genus by it silvery plumage, which was described by the word *argentatus*, the Latin word for 'silver'.

Later developments in DNA profiling tended (annoyingly, sometimes) to shuffle species around different families and genera. Darwin's work on evolutionary biology helps to explain how a single progenitor, for example, a Galápagos finch, could develop in many directions dependent upon factors such as isolation, habitat and food. Both of these developments assisted the work of classification, although these are beyond the scope of this simple work, the purpose of which is to enjoy whatever the study of birds can bring. Perhaps an entry into Greek mythology, into Romantic poetry, into conservation and climate and how these impact on bird populations. Perhaps an interest in the Latin and Greek etymology. By way of an example, the Hoopoe is named by Aristotle as *epops*, but there is no general agreement on the etymology of this word.

Epi is a Greek word meaning 'on' or 'on top of'. **Ops** is the Greek word for an 'eye'. But **psao** is the Greek verb 'to shave'. It's as if Aristotle is asking, 'Where did he get that haircut', or perhaps, 'Look what he's wearing on top'.

I hope this work will bring a little knowledge, a renewed interest and a few chuckles.

Common Hoopoe, *Upupa epops*.

Scientific Names: the Basics

The words listed below may appear in different forms, including as a prefix, a suffix, a full word, or part of a word. This Glossary contains some of the more commonly used words and should provide good background information on the etymology of scientific names for birds.

Glossary of Commonly Used Words

a is a Greek prefix known as the 'alpha privative'. It means 'without', 'lacking'.

anthos (άνθος) refers to the Greek noun for a 'flower'.

ater, atro, etc, from a Latin adjective which means 'black'.

albi, albus, albellus, etc, comes from the Latin adjective for 'white'.

brachos (βραχύς) is a Greek word for 'short'.

cauda is a Latin noun for 'tail'.

ceps a prefix or suffix, comes from the Latin *caput,* meaning 'head'.

chrysos (χρυσός) is the Greek word for 'gold'.

cinereus comes from the Latin word *cineres*, meaning 'ashes'.

caeruleus is a Latin word for 'blue'.

cyanos from the Greek word *kianos* (κυανός) meaning 'blue'.

The aptly named
Eurasian Blue Tit,
Cyanistes caeruleus.

dendron (δένδρον) is a Greek word for 'tree'.

domus is a Latin word for 'house'.

dromos (δρομος) is a Greek word for 'runner'.

flavo, flavescens are the Latin words for 'yellow' and 'yellowish'.

frux is a Latin word for 'fruit'.

fuscus is the Latin word for 'brown' or 'brownish'.

garrulus is a Latin word for 'chattering'.

gula is the Latin word for 'throat'.

haima (αἱμᾰ) is the Greek word for 'blood'.

hydro comes from ὕδωρ, the Greek word for 'water'.

hypo (ὑπό) is a Greek prefix meaning 'under'.

kephale (κεφαλή) is the Greek word for 'head'.

kryptos, kruptos (κρύπτος) is a Greek word meaning 'hidden'.

leuco (λευκό) is the Greek word for 'white'.

morphe (μορφή) is a Greek word meaning 'shape'.

niger is the Latin word for 'black'.

ochros (ὠχρος) is the Greek word for 'yellow' or 'ochre'.

oidos, eidos (εἰδος) comes from the Greek verb 'to see', and means 'looks like'.

ornis (ὄρνις) is the Greek word for 'bird'.

phagein (φαγείν) is a Greek verb meaning 'to eat'.

pódi (πόδι), *pous* (πους), *pes* are Greek words for 'foot'.

polu (πολύ) is a Greek word for 'many'.

platus is the Latin word for' flat'.

pterux (πτέρυξ) is the Greek word for 'wing', so we get *archaeopteryx*, literally 'ancient winged creature', which is best found in the Natural History Museum in London!

rostra is the Latin word for 'bill'.

rhynchos (ρύγχος) is a Greek word meaning 'beak'.

rufa is the Latin word for 'red'.

scopeo (σκοπειν) is the Greek verb 'to see'.

stercora refers to the Latin word for 'excrement'.

tenuis is the Latin word for 'thin'.

viridis is a Latin adjective for 'green'.

vox, vocis is a Latin noun for 'voice'.

xenos (ξένος) is the Greek word for 'strange'.

The all-seeing Eurasian Scops-Owl, *Otus scops*.

Other Common Conventions

Many birds are named after ornithologists or naturalists, for example the Baird's Sandpiper (*Calidris **bairdii***), Gurney's Pitta (*Hydrornis **gurneyi***) and Spix's Macaw (*Cyanopsitta **spixii***) are named after Baird, Gurney and Spix respectively. There are numerous others whose transliteration into Latin often looks clumsy, so the Roseate Tern becomes *Sterna **dougallii***, after McDougall.

Geographical terms such as ***arctica***, ***canadensis*** and ***japonica*** are very commonly found in the scientific names of birds.

Roseate Tern, *Sterna dougallii* – a beautiful bird with an awkward-sounding scientific name.

T

O **Z**

OF BIRD NAMES

Northern Goshawk with Green Woodpecker prey.

Acanthis flammea
Common Redpoll

The genus name was used by Aristotle
to describe a small unidentified bird,
probably a redpoll. The word may share
the same root as *Acanthus,* a generic
term for spiky, thorn-bearing flowers
such as furze and gorse. These bushes are
numerous in the moorland habitat of the
redpoll. *Flammea* refers to the flame-
coloured plumage on the bird's forehead
and breast. Poll is an old English name
for 'head'.

Accipiter gentilis
Northern Goshawk

Accipiter comes from the Latin word,
'to take'. This is a genus of raptors with
short blunt wings, to enable flight through
confined spaces. The tail is long and acts
as a rudder so that the bird can turn
quickly when hunting birds in woods
or forests.

The Northern Goshawk is a large
species and the name is derived from the
Old English word 'Goosehawk'. *Gentilis*
is the Latin word for 'noble'. This was

Acrocephalus paludicola, the innocuous-looking Aquatic Warbler,
leads a private life fit for any soap opera.

A Promiscuous Songster

The marshes in north-east Poland are home to this tiny streak of brown feathers. The Aquatic Warbler lives among an abundance of bird life. The 'tic-toc' of Spotted Crakes and the 'crekking' of Corncrakes is mixed with the song of the male warbler as he announces his availability to females. But no bond develops between the pair – the male Aquatic Warbler has no fixed territory, drifting around looking for females. There are random sexual encounters and the birds are utterly promiscuous. In broods of five or six birds, every fledgling may have a different father.

When a male encounters a female copulation can last for as long as 30 minutes, with the male fending off rivals and producing enough sperm to swamp that of any previous or subsequent males. The aim is to outcompete other males and produce the most descendants.

the bird used for hunting by the nobility. Species such as the Merlin or Eurasian Sparrowhawk would be used by falconers further down the social scale.

– *A. nisus*
Eurasian Sparrowhawk

The species name comes from Greek mythology. *Nisos* was the King of Megara, whom the gods turned into a bird of prey after his daughter betrayed the city to its enemies. He could then take revenge.

Sparrowhawks hunt by surprise attack, using trees or hedges as cover, and fly fast and low for the kill. A bird's presence in a wooded area is often revealed by a plucking point, a stump of tree, for example, with feathers and bones scattered around.

The male is smaller than the female, catching small prey the size of Great Tits and Linnets. The female, around 25 per cent larger, can take prey such as Blackbirds or even Woodpigeons. The division of labour allows a pair to catch almost every kind of garden bird. Their main competitors are cats!

Acrocephalus paludicola
Aquatic Warbler

Acrocephalus comes from two Greek words: *acros* means 'steep' and *kephale* means' head'. The species name comes from two Latin words. *Palus* is the noun for 'swamp', and *colere* is the verb, 'to live'.

– *A. palustris*
Marsh Warbler

Palustris is the Latin word for 'marshy'. The Marsh Warbler is probably the best singer in its genus, noted for its gift of mimicry, but has never been abundant in the UK, where small populations always seem to be on the verge of extinction.

– *A. schoenobaenus*
Sedge Warbler

The word comes from a combination of two ancient Greek words: *schoinos* means 'reed', *baino* means 'to tread'.

The song is varied and chattering, endlessly inventive as other songsters are mimicked. Male Sedge Warblers with the widest repertoire mate with the largest number of females.

– *A. stentoreus*
Clamorous Reed Warbler

In Homer's *The Iliad*, Stentor is the herald whose voice was as loud as 50 men together. The loud chattering of this bird, which is common in the Nile Valley, pays homage to the big-voiced warrior.

Acropternis orthonyx
Ocellated Tapaculo

The genus name comes from three Greek words: *acros* means 'summit' or 'epitome'; *pterux* mean 'wing'; and *ornis* means 'bird'. As the name suggests, this is a 'winged creature with a sublime appearance'.

The specific name comes from *orthos*, a Greek word meaning 'correct' or

Actitis hypoleucos, the Common Sandpiper.

'straight', and *onyx*, a Greek word for a 'fingernail', referring to the fleshy colours found in some examples of the onyx stone. The Latinised form of *onyx* means a 'jewellery box'.

The English name comes from the Latin word *ocellum*, meaning a 'little eye', and refers to the white spots covering the body. *Tapaculo* is an abbreviated form of the Spanish phrase 'cover your bottom', and makes reference the bird's habit of constantly flicking its tail over its back.

This is a skulking bird of thick undergrowth, found in Latin America. The author, on a visit to Ecuador, saw nothing more than a few white spots, then a flash of 'onyx', and the bird was gone, so it stays firmly off the life-list.

Actitis hypoleucos
Common Sandpiper
The binomial classification comes from Ancient Greek. *Actitis* is Greek for a coast-dweller, while *hypo* means 'under', and *leucos* means 'white'. When in danger from a predator, young birds have been known to cling to their parent's body, and fly away to safety.

The Common Sandpiper's tail is constantly in motion, rocking endlessly up and down. The bird flies with quick jerky wing-beats, with the wings held below the horizon.

– *A. macularia*
Spotted Sandpiper
The specific name comes from *maculosus*,

the Latin word for 'spotted' or 'stained'. In the breeding plumage the entire lower half of the body is heavily spotted.

The Spotted Sandpiper breeds in North America and uses a long breeding season to great advantage. Once the eggs are laid the male incubates and the female is free to look for another mate to breed with. The pattern repeats itself as many as four times during the season, and maximises the possible number of young to be reared. The technical term for this process is polyandry, from two Greek words, *polus* meaning 'much', and *andres* meaning 'men'.

Aegithalos caudatus
Long-tailed Tit

Aegithalos is a word used by Aristotle as a generic term for members of the tit family. The etymology is uncertain, though *aegis* is a Greek word for 'protection'. *Cauda* is the Latin name for 'tail'.

The nest is made from four components: lichen, feathers, silk from spider egg cocoons, and moss. The leaves of moss act as hooks, while spider silk provides the loops. This acts to stabilise the nest, so we have a form of Velcro. When nests fail, usually through predation, the failed pair will split and help at the nests of relatives. These tiny birds form roosting flocks in the winter, huddling together for survival through the cold nights.

Sadly, many large raptors are taken from the nest as fledglings and used in the tourist industry, like the Eurasian Black Vulture (*Aegypius monachus*) held aloft by the author in Mongolia. Even if these captive birds escape or are set free, they have lost the ability to hunt or fend for themselves.

Aegypius monachus
Eurasian Black Vulture

The genus name comes from the Greek word used by the writer Aelian (175–235) to describe a bird of prey 'midway between a *gyps* (vulture) and an eagle'. Some commentators thought that the Lammergeier best suited that description.

The species name is a Latin word for a 'monk', and refers to the bald head and ruff-like appearance of the neck feathers.

Agapornis canus
Grey-headed Lovebird

This species inhabits Madagascar and the Comoro Islands. The genus name is derived from *Agape,* which is the Greek word for 'love' (of family, wife, etc). It is distinguished from *philia,* which means 'brotherly love' and *eros,* which means 'sexual love'. Lovebirds are so charming, sociable and attractive, that the three types of love expressed by the Greeks all seem to fit. *Ornis* is the Greek word for 'bird' and the species name *canus* is the Latin word for 'whitish-grey'.

Pair of Mandarin Ducks, *Aix galericulata.*

Aix galericulata
Mandarin Duck

The male has striking plumage. A native of China, the Mandarin Duck has been introduced to the British Isles and breeds by fresh water in forests and woods. *Aix* is a word used by Aristotle to refer to a 'diving bird', and *galericulum* is the Latin word for 'wig'. With head adornments like this, and red side-whiskers, there is little need for a complicated song – a simple 'ack' sound is enough.

The male and female plumages are so different that the Chinese word for the bird, *yuan yang,* is often used to refer to an 'odd couple' or an 'unlikely pair'.

– A. sponsa
Wood Duck

Sponsa is the Latin word for a 'bride'. In the 19th century the numbers of this species, which is also known as the Carolina Duck, declined rapidly, hunted to feed the appetite for spectacularly ornamented ladies hats. As that appetite has waned, its numbers have increased again. The expansion of the North American Beaver population has favoured the fortunes of this duck as the beavers' dams create areas of ideal habitat in forested wetland areas.

Alaemon alaudipes
Greater Hoopoe-Lark

The genus name comes from the Greek word *alemon,* which means 'wanderer'. The specific name comes from the Latin word *alauda,* which means a 'lark'. This is a large, long-legged bird with a downturned bill, able to live in deserts at temperatures of 50°C (122°F). It may shelter in lizard burrows to remain cool and prevent water loss.

Alauda arvensis,
Eurasian Skylark.

Alauda arvensis
Eurasian Skylark

Alauda is the Latin word for 'lark'. *Arvum* is the Latin word for 'ploughed land', a reference to its habitat. The skylark is noted for singing while hovering at a great height. The final plummet to earth is silent. It is a perfect example of a dowdy bird whose plain plumage is more than compensated for by a glorious song.

As the bird disappeared upwards and out of sight, the romantic poet Shelley compared its song to a 'glow-worm', a 'high-born maiden', a 'singer of hymns', a 'cloud of fire'. Soldiers who had dug into the trenches at the battle of the Somme, were heartened to hear the innocent loveliness of its music.

– A. razae
Raso Lark

The specific name is geographical and refers to a tiny outcrop in the Cape Verde Islands, which is the only known home of the Raso Lark.

Cape Verde Adventure

The author visited Raso islet in 2009, but bad weather prevented the boat from landing. Apparently flat calm conditions are unknown and it became clear that setting foot on land would require patience, athleticism and timing. As the boat moved up and down with the motion of the waves, there would only be a second to decide when to make the precarious leap. Once landed, the reward would be the sighting of the endemic Raso Lark, seen only by a very select number of observers. The bird is completely nondescript, and its value for the birdwatcher lies in its rarity. Probably 150 birds are present in total.

In the event, the boatman decided that discretion was the better part of valour. Even from the boat it was clear that this small island, no bigger than 2.7 sq miles (7 sq km), was heaving with seabirds – tropicbirds, shearwaters and storm-petrels packed the rafters.

Alca torda
Razorbill

The etymology is uncertain, although this is the binomial name given to the species by Linnaeus. The Razorbill can dive to a depth of 120m (400ft), and may fly 100km (60 miles) for food. Small schooling fish are captured and swallowed, and delivered in small measures and at regular intervals to the single young chick.

Alcedo atthis
Common Kingfisher

Alcedo is derived from the word 'halcyon'. In Greek mythology *Alcyone* was a goddess punished for her boasting and pride by being reduced to a bird. As an act of compassion, however, she was given seven days each side of the solstice, which were referred to as halcyon days. These were peaceful and calm days when she could raise her young without storm or tempest.

In Greek mythology *Atthis* was a beautiful young woman from the island of Lesvos.

When the Common Kingfisher dives, nictitating membranes close over its eyes to protect them from the water during impact. Like the Osprey, it can compensate for the refraction in the water in order to judge the depth of its prey.

Alle alle
Little Auk

Alle is the Sami (Scandinavian language) for the Long-tailed Duck. It seems that Linnaeus confused the two birds. *Alle* is an onomatopoeic device which imitates the call of the male duck.

This tiny auk falls prey to Arctic Foxes and Glaucous Gulls, and is also eaten as a human food. Up to 500 are stuffed into a seal skin and left underground to ferment for a year, representing a valuable source of food over the bleak winter months.

Amblyornis flavifrons
Golden-fronted Bowerbird

The genus name comes from *ambulare*, the Latin verb meaning 'to walk sedately', and *ornis*, the Greek word for a 'bird'. The species name comes from *flavo*, a Latin word for 'yellow', and *frons*, a Latin word for the 'forehead'. As the genus name suggests, the male spends most of his life on the ground, tending his nest, which is a maypole-like tower of sticks and branches. He walks around his terrain constantly, improving the appearance of his home through the addition of coloured berries.

The Golden-fronted Bowerbird was

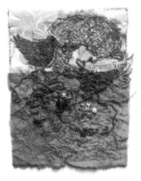

Amblyornis flavifrons, an image of the male Golden-fronted Bowerbird in wool, with an invitation to any prospective female.

Anarhynchus frontalis, the Wrybill showing its uniquely sideways-curved bill.

not photographed until 2005. Its sole habitat is the Foja Mountains in Papua.

Anarhynchus frontalis
Wrybill

The Wrybill is a small plump wader, endemic to New Zealand. It is the only bird whose bill is bent to the side, always to the right. The genus name comes from the Greek *ana,* meaning 'up' or 'again'. It's as if one bend, slightly downward, is not enough.

The specific name comes from *frons,* the Latin word for a 'garland', referring to the capped appearance on the brow.

The 'garland' gives the Wrybill a highly cryptic appearance among the shingle of the riverbed. Here the bent bill can turn over small stones to reveal the larvae, worms and small fish underneath.

Anas acuta
Northern Pintail

The genus name comes from *anas,* the Latin name for a 'duck', and may have originated from *analecta,* meaning 'someone who gathers up waste fragments'. Hunting and shooting birds with lead shot, or the use of lead sinkers by anglers, can cause lead poisoning in dabbling ducks as this 'gathering up' of fragments may lead to the ingestion of

Anas clypeata, or the 'shield-billed sifter of waste fragments'.
More commonly known as the Northern Shoveler.

poisonous matter. Therefore in many countries, by law, all shot used for waterfowl must be non-toxic and free of lead.

Acuta is the Latin word for 'sharp', and refers to the pointed tail of the male in breeding plumage. As with other dabbling ducks, the female is a dowdy brown colour and lacks the rich chocolate and white of the male's head.

– *A. carolinensis*
Green-winged Teal
The specific term is geographical, this being the North American counterpart to the Eurasian Teal, from which the male can be distinguished by a vertical rather than horizontal white stripe on the flank. Females of the two species appear virtually identical to the human eye.

– *A. clypeata*
Northern Shoveler
Clypeus is the Latin word for a 'shield'. The bill is huge and spatulate, equipped with comb-like structures that act as sieves to trap crustaceans and plankton. A flock of shovelers may form a dense pack and circle rapidly in the water, with their motion creating a funnel which brings food to the surface.

Anhinga. Look at the neck and you can see how the this family gained its collective colloquial name of 'snakebird'.

– *A. crecca*
Eurasian Teal

The specific name given by Linnaeus refers to the call of the bird, which makes a 'crec crec' sound. In English, 'teal' is a greenish-blue colour.

– *A. platyrhynchos*
Mallard

Literally, 'the duck with the flat bill'. *Platos* is the Greek word for 'flat'. *Rhynchos* is the Greek word for a 'beak'.

The Mallard is the main ancestor of most domestic ducks. The bird has a flexible genetic code, which gives it a vast interbreeding capability. The genes which decide plumage colour are also flexible, and birds kept in aviaries or as pets show a variety of hues and shades.

Anhinga anhinga
Anhinga

This is a Neotropical bird, whose name comes from the word *anhinga,* a demonic spirit among the Tupi people of South America.

– *A. rufa*
African Darter

Rufa is the Latin word for 'red'. 'Darter' refers to the birds' manner of procuring food, as they impale fish with their dagger-like bills. After they have stabbed their prey, they toss the food into the air, catch it, and swallow the fish head-first. This prevents spines from sticking in their throat.

Anous tenuirostris
Lesser Noddy

The genus name comes from Greek words. *A* is the alpha privative, and means 'missing'. *Nous* is the word for 'mind'. The poor bird is considered to be 'simple-minded' since it allows itself to be caught so easily.

The specific name comes from two Latin words. *Tenuis* means 'thin', and *rostrum* means 'bill'.

This noddy is found in the Indian Ocean, with the largest colonies in the Seychelles. It feeds in typical tern-like fashion, by picking small fish and crustaceans from the surface of the water. The thin bill (*tenuirostris*) is perfectly adapted for this purpose.

– Anser anser
Greylag Goose

Anser is the Latin word for 'goose', so this species is literally 'goose goose'.

This noisy bird has the same clamorous speech as its farmyard derivative: honking and hissing in an aggressive posture. There is a legend that the sacred geese in Rome alerted soldiers on the Capitoline Hill when the Gauls attacked in 390 CE.

– A. fabalis
Bean Goose

Faba is the Latin word for 'broad bean', and refers to birds of this species eating through the stubble of bean fields.

Anthropoides virgo
Demoiselle Crane

The genus name comes from Greek words: *anthropos* means 'human being', *oides* means 'looks like'. *Virgo* is the Latin name for a 'virgin'. The English name uses the Old French word for an unmarried woman.

This elegant bird breeds in Eurasia and winters in Africa and the Indian Subcontinent. In India it is called the 'Koonj'. Beautiful girls are often named 'Koonj' as they might resemble the long, thin shape of the bird.

The word 'Koonj' also refers to someone who has travelled, like the bird, a long and dangerous journey. Demoiselle Cranes migrate across the Himalayas, reaching heights of 8,000m (26,000ft). Many die from hunger or predation by eagles.

Anthus pratensis
Meadow Pipit

Anthus is the Latin name for a 'small grassland bird', but probably originates from the Greek *anthos*, meaning flower. *Pratum* is the Latin name for 'meadow'. The word 'pipit' comes from the call note.

– A. hodgsoni
Olive-backed Pipit

Also known as Hodgson's Pipit and named after Brian Houghton Hodgson (1800–1894), a British-born naturalist resident in India and Nepal. Hodgson brought a grand total of 10,499 bird

In this case the Greylag Goose, *Anser anser*, goslings have imprinted on the correct parent.

A Case of Malimprinting

In a series of experiments with Greylag Geese, Konrad Lorenz (1903–1989), the Austrian psychologist, noticed that young goslings, newly hatched in the absence of their mother, would form an attachment with the first person or creature they saw. A brood of goslings followed him everywhere, in the water as he swam, in his canoe, and on dry land. His image, the first they had seen, had been 'imprinted' on their minds. The science of ethology – the study of animal behaviour – is used more and more as a tool for increasing our understanding of human behaviour.

skins from India and Nepal to the British Museum. Among them were 124 species which were previously undescribed. These were later transferred to the Natural History Museum.

Hodgson trained Indian friends to paint birds, being attentive to the most minute details, including tarsi, nasal orifices and supercilia, and ensuring that they are faithfully rendered in art. His interests were wide and varied. Darwin wrote of his ability to train the Indian Wild Dog or Dhole, making them as intelligent and as fond of him as ordinary domestic pets.

Aptenodytes forsteri
Emperor Penguin

The genus name comes from Ancient Greek. *A* means 'without', *pterux* means 'wing', and *dytes* means 'diver'.

Georg Forster (1754–1794) was a German naturalist who was invited to join Captain Cook's second expedition to the Pacific. Forster's drawings include some of birds which are now extinct, for example the Tanna Ground Dove.

Emperor Penguins belong in the Antarctic and their statistics are impressive. Males stand 1.2m (4ft) high and during incubation they eat nothing for two months. A young female was recorded swimming underwater at a depth of 535m (1,755ft). In extreme cold, when temperatures fall to -60°C (-76°F), birds huddle together with youngsters in the middle. The adults then shuffle around,

so that the warm centre and the cold exterior are shared equally.

Courtship begins in April, when the ice has thickened enough to support thousands of penguins. Males swagger around the colony with exaggerated head movements, singing their short song and looking impressive. If a male succeeds he will attract a mate, then it's time to 'p p pick up a penguin'.

Apteryx australis
Southern Brown Kiwi

Apteryx comes from two Greek words. *A* means 'without', and *pterux* is the Greek word for 'wing'. *Australis* is a Latin word for 'south'. Among bird species, only kiwis have nostrils at the tips of their long bills. These are sensitive and the birds can locate worms and insects underground due to their heightened sense of smell. For all its unique features the kiwi is no 'Pavaroti' in the music department. A single repeated screech is all that any listener may expect.

Apus apus
Common Swift

A is the alpha privative in Greek and suggests that something is lacking. *Pus* derives from *pes*, the Latin for a foot. These are the most aerial of all birds, living entirely on insects caught on narrow, scythe-like wings.

Outside the breeding season the bird lives entirely on the wing, and early observers thought that the feet were missing. For the first two years of its life the swift is entirely airborne. The first contact with any object larger than its prey will be the moment when two birds embrace in the air, and a new generation is begun.

Tiny geolocators fixed to the bird, weighing just a few grams, enable scientists to track smaller and smaller birds. These miniature devices have recorded swifts ascending to a height of 2 miles (3km), to sleep safely on the wing. *Apus* seems the perfect word for a bird with such an ability.

Aquila audax
Wedge-tailed Eagle

Aquilus is the Latin word for 'dark in colour'. *Audax* is the Latin meaning both 'courageous' and 'foolhardy'.

In November 2016 the Sydney Morning Herald reported that these birds were doing battle with drones used by mining companies, and had knocked nine out of the sky!

– A. chrysaetos
Golden Eagle

Chrysos is the Greek word for gold.

The Golden Eagle is much regarded in falconry. The Eurasian subspecies is used to hunt and kill foxes and wolves which prey on sheep. In Kazakhstan the birds are taken from their nests as young and live with the families of hunters. When hunting on horseback the birds are hooded until a wolf or fox is spotted, then the hood is removed and the bird attacks and kills at great speed. After five years the eagle is released back into the wild and soars away to freedom.

At one time it was thought that the eagle could look directly into the sun, and the bird achieved a sort of mystical status. The standard of the Roman legions bore an eagle, which was carried into battle. The gold colour (*chrysos*) suggested power over the enemy. In heraldry it features in the coat of arms of many a royal house.

– A. clanga
Greater Spotted Eagle

The species name comes from *clangae*, the Greek word for a 'scream', and refers to the dog-like *yelp* of the bird. This species breeds in wooded country in northern Eurasia. It is highly migratory, flying south during winter, when large numbers gather at refuse dumps in Oman. Here observers can hone their identification skills among Greater Spotted, Lesser Spotted, Booted and Steppe Eagles, and a variety of vultures. Waste disposal sites are major stepping-stones for migratory birds, offering plenty of edible materials in an otherwise arid landscape.

Ardea cinerea
Grey Heron

The genus name comes from *arduus*, a Latin word for 'lofty'. The specific name comes from *cineres*, the Latin word for 'ashes', and makes reference to the bird's grey plumage.

No other heron matches *Ardea goliath* in terms of its giant stature.

This species was once considered a delicacy at the dinner table, and there is a record of four hundred herons being served at the consecration of Archbishop George Neville (1432–1476) in the year 1465.

Grey Herons have adapted well to urban living. Their heronries, with closely packed nests, can often be found in city parks. They have even been observed entering zoos and stealing food left out for penguins and seals, while every trout fishery has protective netting to prevent theft.

– A. goliath
Goliath Heron

A giant bird named after the Philistine warrior Goliath. In the Bible narrative he is brought to his death by a slingshot from the boy David. This heron is found in Sub-Saharan Africa and south-west Asia, and is usually solitary.

Ardeotis arabs
Arabian Bustard

The genus name comes from *ardea,* the Latin word for a 'heron', and *otiosus*, the Latin word for 'slow-moving' or 'lazy'. The species name comes from *arabis*, the Greek word for 'sandy soil'.

As the etymology suggests this is a large and slow-moving bird, and it is in rapid decline due primarily to hunting by humans. A variety of falcons are taken into the desert and released when bustards

Arenaria interpres, although the Ruddy Turnstone's scientific name was 'misinterpreted' by Linnaeus.

are sighted. Hunting by foot and camel has been replaced by hunting with four-wheel drive vehicles, and these large and slow birds (*tarda*), which are visible from a distance, have little chance of escape. What was called the 'sport of kings' has become a sorry and unsustainable tale of carnage.

Arenaria interpres
Ruddy Turnstone

Arenaria is a Latin term for 'sand shore'. *Interpres* can be literally translated as 'interpreter', although this name is based on a misnomer. The species was named by Linnaeus, but he confused the turnstone with the Common Redshank (*Tringa totanus*), which goes by the Swedish name of *tolk*, or 'interpreter' in English.

As the common name suggests, the bird turns over stones to expose hidden molluscs, worms and insects. When feeding collectively, dominant birds show a lowered tail and hunched appearance, so as to frighten immature birds and feed more successfully.

Asio flammeus
Short-eared Owl

A very widespread owl, which is often seen hunting during the day. *Asio* is the Latin word for 'owl'. *Flammeus* means 'brightly coloured'. As with other owls, hard-to-digest parts of the prey, such as bones, feathers and fur, are quickly regurgitated as pellets. These pellets are fascinating to study but should be microwaved beforehand, especially in schools, as they have been known to contain toxic matter. One study shows two cases of salmonella poisoning in schools as a result of examining owl pellets.

Athene cunicularia, the Burrowing Owl, at the entrance to its burrow.

Athene cunicularia
Burrowing Owl

Athene is the Greek goddess of wisdom, often symbolised by an owl.

The specific name comes from the Latin word *cuniculus*, which means a 'rabbit' or an 'underground passage'.

The Burrowing Owl is found in open landscapes in the Americas. The bird has noticeably long legs, giving an advantage when on the lookout for prey or predators, and enabling it to sprint after prey. When threatened the owl will retreat into its burrow and make sounds like a rattlesnake.

The nest is often lined with cattle dung, to control the microclimate and to attract edible flies.

– *A. noctua*
Little Owl

Noctua resonates with 'nocturnal'. It was once thought that the call of the owl heralded the death of Julius Caesar. We might imagine the reprimand of Caesar as his assassins struck: '*Et tu, Brute*'. '*Et tu, Athene noctua*'.

Atlantisia rogersi
Inaccessible Island Rail

The genus name is geographical, and the species name refers to the sailor and naturalist Rogers, who first described this isolated South Atlantic outpost.

Aulacorhynchus prasinus
Emerald Toucanet

The genus name is taken from two Greek words. *Aulacos* refers to 'royalty', and *rynchos* is the word for 'nose'. *Prasinus* is the Latin word for 'green'.

Despite the size of their bills, these are not heavy as they are formed from keratin, the same substance as human nails. The bill seems to perform various functions, including peeling fruit, intimidating predators, attracting a mate, and as a heat regulator.

These lovely birds are found in Central America and are often kept as pets, although they require a lot of space and plenty of fruit. The rewards for the keeper are based on the bird's personality, as the toucanet interacts playfully with humans and is quick to learn tricks.

Aythya collaris
Ring-necked Duck

The scientific name comes from ancient Greek. *Aithuia* was an unidentified duck mentioned by Aristotle.

Collaris is the Latin word for 'collared'. It is perhaps not the most obvious name for the species. The cinnamon neck-ring is difficult to see, but on the other hand the two white rings at the base and tip of the grey bill are very clear.

– A. fuligula
Tufted Duck

Fuligo is the Latin word for '*soot*', and *gula* is the Latin word for 'throat'.

Aulacorhynchus prasinus, the Emerald Toucanet.

Island Dwarfism

At 18cm (7in) in length, the Inaccessible Island Rail is the smallest flightless bird in the world. Its island home rises 300m (1,000ft) from the ocean on sheer cliffs, making access very difficult. No human lives there permanently. Around 5,000 of these tiny creatures roam freely on their paradise island, feeding on insects and seeds. Their tiny size is an example of 'island dwarfism'. Understood in layman's language, it seems that one strategy for creatures in restricted surroundings with limited resources to survive is by becoming smaller. At the moment the island is free of predators, but if a cat, rat, dog, stoat, or any species which competes for food were to arrive, the rail's status might change completely.

Balaeniceps rex, the 'whale-headed king', better known as the Shoebill.

Balaeniceps rex
Shoebill

The genus name comes from two Latin words. *Ballaena* means 'whale' and *caput* is the word for a 'head'.

The species name comes from the Latin word *rex*, for a 'king'.

The whale-headed bird is truly the 'king of the swamps', standing at around 140cm (55in). Surveys among keen birders have seen this prehistoric-looking creature listed as one of the top five 'must see' bird species in Africa, and the tourism industry benefits from the eagerness of birders to travel long distances for a sighting of a special bird.

The Shoebill's main diet is lungfish, for which it will wait stock still, and then attack with speed and ferocity. The sharp hooked bill holds the most slippery fish and offers them no chance of escape.

And yet, the Shoebill was chosen as the ugliest creature on the earth according to the *Beastly Countdown* television series on Animal Planet.

Bartramia longicauda
Upland Sandpiper

While most of its relatives rarely stray far from water, the Upland Sandpiper has made his home in the grasslands of North America, where it is sometimes known as the 'shorebird of the prairie'. The specific name comes from two Latin words: *longus*, means 'long', and *cauda* means 'tail'.

The *genus* is named after the American naturalist William Bartram (1739–1823). Another common name for the bird is Bartram's Sandpiper, and this name was popularised by the naturalist Alexander Wilson (1766–1813) in gratitude to Bartram, who had taught him the rudiments of ornithology and natural history illustration. Bartram wrote in his diaries that when he was studying the flora of Georgia, he met a member of the Seminole tribe who had vowed to kill the first white man he met, but was disarmed by Bartram's charm and kindness. His botanical paintings are works of great precision and beauty.

Bombycilla cedrorum
Cedar Waxwing

Bombycilla is a made-up Latin word for 'silky tail', which was coined by the French naturalist Louis Vieillot (1748–1830).

Vieillot worked mostly in the Americas. His great interest was taxonomy, a science which allocates different classes of birds to their order, family, genus and specific differences,

and 32 species of flora and fauna in the Americas bear his name. His influence has also spread to other parts of the world, with, for example, the Vieillot's Barbet (*Lybius vieilloti*) in Africa.

Cedrorum is a Latin word, which means 'belonging to cedar trees'. This species inhabits North and Central America. These birds are highly sociable and rarely seen singly, except perhaps when they appear in Britain as extremely rare visitors.

Flocks of these birds will descend and feast voraciously on berry-laden trees. If the fruit is over-ripe, Cedar Waxwings can become drunk on the fermented juices, and may fly in erratic patterns, or collapse on the ground until the effect wears off and they 'sober up'.

– *B. garrulus*
Bohemian Waxwing

Garrulus is the Latin word for 'chattering'.

The English name 'waxwing' refers to the red tips on some of the flight feathers, which have a wax-like appearance.

'Bohemian' refers to the nomadic nature of this species. The adjective fits well as the birds travel great distances to find food. When they arrive in Britain during winter they feed exclusively on berries, attracting attention with their soft trilling calls.

The Bohemian Waxwing is a great beauty, and often easy to photograph due to its generally confiding nature. In spring the birds add insects to their diet, and

Bohemian Waxwings, *Bombycilla garrulus*.

nest together in groups beside good food sources in northern forests.

– B. japonica
Japanese Waxwing

The word *japonica* is a geographical term. Japanese Waxwings lack the row of wax-like tips on the feathers. Birds which appear in Europe are probably escapees from cages.

Botaurus stellaris
Great Bittern

Botaurus comes from two words. *Buteo* is the Latin for 'hawk'. *Taurus* is the Latin for 'ox' or 'bull'. The birds fly with their heads retracted. When startled the bittern adopts a classic pose, with bill pointed upwards, blending in well with its reedy surroundings.

The specific name comes from *stella*, the Latin word for a 'star', and refers to the spangled markings on the wing.

The Great Bittern is a stealth predator, standing motionless until prey appears. It then uses its bill, which is long, sharp and deadly, to spear a frog or fish.

The genus name is apt as the call-note of the male is likened to the bellowing of a bull (in Latin, *taurus*) and can be heard 3 miles (5km) away. The sound is made by expelling air from the oesophagus.

Branta canadensis
Canada Goose

Branta is an Old Norse word
meaning 'burnt' or 'blackened'.

The specific name *canadensis*
is a geographical term.

The pattern of flight in the 'V'
formation has been much studied.
The leading position, which consumes
the most energy, is rotated to share
the burden.

– B. leucopsis
Barnacle Goose

Leucopsis comes from two Greek
words. *Leuko* means 'white', and *opsis*
means 'faced'.

The myth that Barnacle Geese were
born from goose barnacle shells persisted
until the 18th century. In appearance the
shell does seem goose-like with its long
curved neck. Some authors even claimed
to have seen the very process of birth,
with tiny geese emerging from the shells.

In County Kerry, Ireland, Catholics
were forbidden to eat meat on Fridays,
but could eat this bird because it
counted as a fish.

– B. ruficollis
Red-breasted Goose

Ruficollis comes from two Latin words. *Rufus* means 'red' and *collis* means 'necked'. This is a small and timid goose with limited natural defence mechanisms. To protect themselves from Arctic Foxes, they nest close to large birds of prey such as Peregrine Falcons and Snowy Owls. When these raptors change nesting sites, the Red-breasted Geese follow.

Branta canadensis,
Canada Geese, in 'V' formation.

Canada Geese: Loved or Unloved

These large geese are successful in setting up home in altered environments such as golf courses, parks and other places for human recreation. They are big birds with gargantuan appetites and are often seen as a pest species when they eat their way through crop fields. Canada Geese will attack humans who approach too close to the nest, inflicting scratches and bites. They fly high and have collided with aircraft, for example in 1995 an E-3 Sentry aircraft struck a flock of geese and crashed, killing all 24 members on board.

Add to that the bacteria in the birds' large droppings, the noise of a flock and their aggressive behaviour towards humans when begging, and it is little wonder that they are not everyone's favourite bird.

The huge Eagle Owl, *Bubo bubo*.

Bubo bubo
Eurasian Eagle-Owl

The genus name is a Latin word meaning 'owl'. The word *bubo* has affinities with various Latin words referring to cattle, probably because of the 'hoot' sound made by some species in this genus which is reminiscent of a lowing bovine.

These are huge birds, and the wing-span of a female can measure 188cm (6ft 2in). Skeletal remains suggest the bird bred in Britain as recently as the 1st century AD. Recently a number of escapees have bred successfully in Britain.

A Hero

In June 2007 a Eurasian Eagle-Owl landed on the pitch during an international football match between Finland and Belgium in Helsinki. It flew off shortly after Jonatan Johansson scored for the home team in a 2–0 win. This charismatic bird was considered to have inspired the team to victory and was later named 'Helsinki Citizen of the Year'.

Bubulcus ibis, Cattle Egret 'guarding the beef'.

– B. scandiacus
Snowy Owl

Scandiacus is a geographical name, as the species inhabits the Northern Circumpolar region. The English name refers to the 'snowy' plumage, which offers perfect camouflage in the bird's icy habitat. The Snowy Owl hunts by using a 'sit and wait' method, and needs to consume around 10 rodents every day just to stay alive. The male defends the nest with great vigour and other birds such as Snow Geese will nest close to the owls, in order to give themselves protection against predators such as foxes and crows.

Bubulcus ibis
Cattle Egret

The genus name *Bubulcus* is the Latin name for 'herdsman', due to the Cattle Egret's association with cattle. *Ibis* originally referred to another bird, the Sacred Ibis. Commonly seen perched on the backs of cattle, the Cattle Egret is popular with ranchers as is helps to control ticks and flies. The French name is very descriptive: 'Héron garde-boeufs'.

A Lonely Bachelor

Snowy Owls set up an isolated breeding outpost on Fetlar, Shetland, from 1967–1975. This was wonderful for the tourist industry and bed and breakfast was offered in every other house. Twitchers, photographers and curious people, including the author, all made the trip north to pay homage to these lovely creatures. Over time the dominant male chased away any young males who visited, and when he died only females were left, with at one time as many as nine on the island. With no prospect of a mate, they eventually went elsewhere.

The range of the Cattle Egret has expanded rapidly in recent decades. Entirely unknown in the Americas until the late 19th century, it became established in South America from the 1930s and reached North America in the 1940s and 1950s. The bird is now widespread and abundant across the Americas.

A great opportunist,
the Cattle Egret will
not only follow cattle
which stir up insects,
but also tractors and
farm machinery which
do the same. The bird
will even fly towards fires, to feast on
grasshoppers, small rodents and other
evacuees escaping the flames.

Bucephala albeola showing its 'bull-shaped head' to full effect.

Bucanetes githagineus
Trumpeter Finch

Bucanetes is the Greek for 'trumpeter'.
Githago is the Latin word for the flower
'corncockle', a toxic plant which was
recently rediscovered growing near
Sunderland, having previously been
considered extinct in the UK.

The connection with the bird?
Coenraad Temminck (1778–1858),
the Dutch naturalist who gave the
Trumpeter Finch its scientific name,
wrongly believed that its name was
derived from this plant.

Bucephala albeola
Bufflehead

Bucephala is a genus of ducks found in
the Northern Hemisphere. *Bous* is the
Greek word for 'bull' and *kephale* is the
Greek word for 'head'. Each of the three
species in the genus has a high, stout, bull-
like forehead, in particular the Bufflehead.
When the male Bufflehead puffs out its
head feathers, the 'buffalo' effect is more
pronounced.

Albeola comes from
alba, the Latin word
for 'white'.

The small size of
this American duck
has evolved to fit
neatly into the nesting
cavity of the Northern Flicker, a type of
woodpecker. When a flock of Buffleheads
dives for food, one bird often remains
on the surface to keep a look out for
predators.

– B. clangula
Common Goldeneye

Clango is the Latin verb, 'to make a peal
sound', or simply 'to make a noise'.
The latter use is more fitting here, as
the notes are mostly guttural and sharp.
The Common Goldeneye nests in trees
and takes readily to bird boxes.

– B. islandica
Barrow's Goldeneye

Islandica is a geographical term. Barrow's
Goldeneye is a bird of Iceland and the
mountain lakes of western America.

The English name commemorates
Sir John Barrow (1764–1848), who was
born in Cumbria and joined a whaling
expedition to Greenland at the young
age of 16. Later, when he worked in the
Admiralty, he promoted Arctic voyages
of discovery.

The species appears in British waters
from time to time, perhaps sometimes
as an escapee from private collections.

Buceros bicornis, the Great Hornbill.

There's a rule among birdwatchers: if it comes to bread, it's probably an escapee.

Buceros bicornis
Great Hornbill
This is the largest of the several species of hornbill that can be found in south Asia. *Buceros* comes from the Latin for 'ox-headed', and *bicornis* comes from the Latin for 'two' (*bi*) and 'horned' (*cornu*). The casque is hollow, to reduce the weight in flight.

Traditionally tribal people used various parts of this hornbill for ceremonial purposes, with the feathers used as a head dress and the casque for ornamentation.

There is a record of a captive Great Hornbill which lived for 50 years in a cage in the office of Walter Willard (died 1952), a naturalist in India. When the bird expired some suggested he had swallowed a piece of wire, although he had already drunk wine and eaten a cigar with no ill effects. Most people who knew the bird thought he had died of a broken heart as Mr Willard had recently passed away.

Bulweria bulwerii
Bulwer's Petrel
The species is named after the Reverend James Bulwer (1794–1879), an Anglican priest and a member of the Linnean

Society, who collected a single specimen of this unknown bird on the Madeiran islands. The word petrel makes reference to Saint Peter, who is described as 'walking on the water' in the Gospel of Saint Matthew. It is perhaps more apt for the smaller storm-petrels, which seem to dance over the water's surface.

Buphagus erythrorhynchus
Red-billed Oxpecker

The genus name of this sub-Saharan bird comes from the Latin word *bos*, meaning a cow, and the Greek verb *fagein*, meaning 'to eat'.

The species name comes from the Greek word for 'reddening'. The Latin derivation *erubescere* means 'to blush', and refers to the colour of the bill. *Rhynchus* is the Greek word for 'nose'.

As the name suggests, the oxpecker feeds on ticks and flies found on large mammals such as cattle. One bird can consume around 100 blood-engorged ticks every day. They will also feed on mucus, saliva and blood where the animal has been wounded.

The nest is in a tree hole, lined with hair plucked from livestock.

Burhinus oedicnemus
Eurasian Stone-curlew

The genus name comes from *bous*, the Greek word for an 'ox', and *rhis*, a Greek noun for 'nose'.

The species name comes from *oudio*, the Greek verb 'to swell', and *kneme*, the

Greek word for 'leg'. The leg joints are sturdy and give the name 'thick-knee'.

The stone-curlew is rather inactive during the day, and prefers to hunt at night, when the large yellow eyes maximise whatever light is available. The English name makes reference to the nocturnal call, which resembles that of a curlew, and 'stone' refers to its preferred rocky habitat.

Buteo buteo
Common Buzzard

Buteo is a genus of raptors with variable plumage. *Buteo* is the Latin word for a 'hawk'. The call note can sound like the 'miaow' of a cat, or the 'mew' of a gull.

The plumage of the nominate race is extremely variable, between mostly white and very dark brown.

– *B. lagopus*
Rough-legged Buzzard

Lagopus comes from two Greek words. *Lago* is the Greek word for 'hare', and *pous* is the Greek word for 'foot'. The 'feathered feet' are well adapted to the freezing conditions of the taiga and tundra. The talons are smaller than those of *Buteo buteo*, reflecting the smaller size of the prey, which includes lemmings, voles and small passerines such as Snow Buntings.

Remarkably there is some evidence that the birds can 'see' the scent marks left by voles, which are only visible to humans when using an ultraviolet (UV) detector. Moreover, studies by Bennett and Cuthill

Butorides striatus striking a classic hunting pose.

(1994) suggest that up to 30 species of raptors which hunt during the day may have ultraviolet vision.

Butorides striatus
Striated Heron

An Old World and South American heron. *Butorides* comes from the Greek word *oides*, meaning 'resembling', and *butor* is the Middle English name for the Bittern. *Striatus* is the Latin word for 'streaked'.

The Striated Heron will sometimes use a lure, perhaps a feather or leaf placed on the surface of the water, and pick up fish that come to investigate.

– B. sundevalli
Lava Heron

The Lava Heron is endemic to the Galápagos Islands, where its slate-grey plumage blends in well with the hardened lava. The bird is named after the Swedish zoologist Carl Jakob Sundevall

(1801–1875), who introduced two new words into the ornithological vocabulary: 'altricial' and 'precocial'. *Altrix* is the Latin word for 'nurse', and altricial birds are born naked and blind, depending upon their parents for food. *Prae* is the Latin word for 'early', and *coquere* is a Latin verb meaning 'to ripen', so precocial birds are those already covered in down when born, and able to leave the nest almost immediately. All members of the heron family are *altricial*, born blind and naked, and only able to leave the nest when adult-sized.

– B. virescens
Green Heron

Viridus is the Latin for 'green'. This is a bird of North and Central America. There are several plumage differences among the various populations, and migratory birds have longer wings, but there is disagreement among ornithologists as to subspecies distinctions.

Sulphur-crested Cockatoo, *Cacatua galerita.*

Cacatua galerita
Sulphur-crested Cockatoo
The genus name comes from *Cacaturio*, a Latin verb meaning 'to evacuate the bowels'. The Dutch naturalist Coenraad Temminck (1778–1858), who gave the species its scientific name, was probably referring to the damage done by the bird's droppings.

The species name comes from *galerum*, a Latin word for 'hat' or 'wig', and makes reference to the sulphur-coloured crest.

Sulphur-crested Cockatoos are very numerous in some Australian cities and are often considered as pests. They are also popular as pets, interacting well with humans, and can be taught to speak.

Calandrella brachydactyla
Greater Short-toed Lark
Calandrella is a diminutive of *calandros*, which refers to the much larger Calandra Lark.

Brachus is the Greek word for 'short', *daktyl* is the Greek word for 'toe' or 'finger'.

There is much genetic variation within the species, with several subspecies recognised, some of which could potentially be 'split' in future.

Calidris acuminata
Sharp-tailed Sandpiper

Calidris is a Greek word used by Aristotle for some grey-coloured seashore birds.

Acuminata comes from the Latin word for 'pointed', referring to the tail.

This species breeds in Siberia and winters south to Australia and New Zealand.

A white winter-plumaged Sanderling (*Calidris alba*) in full 'clockwork toy' mode.

– *C. alba*
Sanderling

Alba is the Latin word for 'white', relating to the bird's winter plumage. In spring the upperparts are brown and the face and throat become brick-red.

The Sanderling rushes madly at the edge of the surf, behaving like a clockwork toy, catching its tiny prey between the ebb and flow of the water.

– *C. bairdii*
Baird's Sandpiper

This American wader is named after Spencer Fullerton Baird (1823–1887). Baird was a naturalist of enormous energy, making many of his expeditions on foot, for example in 1887 he walked a total of 2,100 miles (3,380km). His interests included reptiles, birds and fish, although after a meeting with Audubon, the great American bird artist, his interests turned primarily to birds. Five species of birds are named after Baird: a sandpiper, woodpecker, trogon, flycatcher and sparrow. Baird is remembered as a collector of specimens, and the number of specimens in the Smithsonian Institute rose from 60,000 to 2 million during his time as Secretary.

– *C. canutus*
Red Knot

The etymology is uncertain. *Canutus* resonates with the story of King Canute (995–1035), who allegedly sat at the water's edge, clothed in his royal garments, to show his fawning courtiers that he had no power to command the tides. According to Henry of Huntingdon, King Canute wanted to show that secular power was vain compared to the power of God.

The Critically Endangered Spoon-billed Sandpiper showing its unique spatulate bill.

– C. ferruginea
Curlew Sandpiper

The species name comes from *ferratus*, the Latin word for 'iron', while *rugo* is the Latin word for 'red'. Numbers of Curlew Sandpipers fluctuate according to the breeding success of lemmings. In poor lemming years, predators such as skuas and Snowy Owls will take waders instead.

– C. melanotos
Pectoral Sandpiper

Melane is a Greek word for black, and refers to the dark and heavily streaked breast. Both male and female Pectoral Sandpipers are promiscuous and will mate with multiple partners.

– C. pygmaea
Spoon-billed Sandpiper

Pygmaea is a reference to the bird's diminutive size. This is a Critically Endangered species with a unique spatulate bill which is swung from side to side as it feeds. An artificial incubation programme at Slimbridge, UK, since 2011 has released over 100 birds back into the wild, representing a significant contribution for a species which may have a wild population of as few as 250 individuals.

With an enormous fan club, the 'spoonie' seems to pull every emotional string. As its migration flight path was monitored recently, an army of adoring admirers followed every wing-beat from Russia to Thailand. On social media, a typical tweet read: 'Love and kisses to ET. Safe journey to you, little one'.

Calonectris borealis
Cory's Shearwater

The genus name comes from the Greek words '*kalos*', which means good, and '*nectris*', which means swimmer.

Borealis is the Latin word for 'northern'.

The Cory's Shearwater nests in crevices or rabbit burrows, and visits the nest at night to avoid detection by predators.

Charles B. Cory (1857–1921), after whom the bird is named, came from a wealthy family, and had the money and leisure time to travel all over the Americas and amass a huge collection of skins, around 19,000, along with 600 books on ornithology. His own writing on birds was prolific and extremely detailed.

Cory also competed in the 1904 Summer Olympics as a golfer, perhaps looking for new species on the golf course, where of course you can find birdies, eagles and albatrosses! He withdrew before the final round.

Camarhynchus pallidus
Woodpecker Finch

The genus name comes from *camella*, the Latin name for a 'goblet' or 'cup', and refers to the shape of the stubby beak, and

A close encounter with the European Nightjar, *Caprimulgus europaeus*.

the Greek word *rhynchos*, meaning a 'nose'.

Pallidus is the Latin word for 'pale'.

Whoever used the term 'birdbrain' to describe someone lacking grey matter had never heard of the Galápagos Woodpecker Finch. The tongue is too short to dislodge prey such as grubs from tree hollows, so a tool is used instead. A cactus spine will do the job perfectly. Grubs are eased out of hollows and the cactus spine is carried from branch to branch. Woodpecker Finches have been seen cutting off parts of the spine to make the tool more manageable.

Caprimulgus europaeus
European Nightjar

Capri resonates with words like Capricorn. *Capra* is the 'nanny goat' in Latin. *Mulgere* is the Latin verb 'to milk'. The traditional old name for the nightjar is 'goatsucker', as country folks once thought that this night-flyer subsisted on the milk from goats.

These crepuscular beauties become active as dusk falls. The wings are stiff and the flight is hawk-like as they drift through the darkness, while huge eyes make the most of any light available in order to locate insect prey. Wear a white hat when they emerge and they will sometimes fly close enough to clip your head – you won't get a better view!

Casuarius casuarius, the Southern Cassowary, cuts an imposing figure in the rainforest.

– C. aegyptius
Egyptian Nightjar

The specific name is geographical. This bird inhabits arid regions from North Africa to Central Asia. Its pale plumage blends in with its sandy surroundings.

Nightjars of many species often sit in the middle of the road between bouts of feeding on moths, and the reflections of their eyes can be picked out in the beam of a torch or a car's headlights.

Casuarius casuarius
Southern Cassowary

The scientific name is the Latinised word for *kesuari*, the bird's name in Malay, and makes reference to the lethal claws. These gigantic birds of the rainforests of north-east Australia, New Guinea and neighbouring islands are quite able to kill a person or a dog if they are cornered.

The sharp talons on the centre toe have traditionally been used in New Guinea to make spear-heads. There are numerous accounts of 'bird-on-human' attacks, sometimes because they are fed by tourists, then angered when feeding is withdrawn. If chased or attacked advice suggests that the best defence is to raise an arm in order to appear taller.

The bare skin on the head and neck becomes deeper blue as the bird becomes excited or angry. After laying a clutch of eggs the female abandons the nest, leaving the male to hatch and rear the young; she then searches for other males in order to repeat the process.

Attack by *Catharacta skua*, Great Skua.

Catharacta skua
Great Skua

Catharacta comes from the Greek word *catharos*, which means 'pure', referring to the cleansing (scavenging) habits of the bird.

The English name comes from *Skúvoy*, a Faroese island where the bird is plentiful.

Visitors to any breeding sites will be familiar with the Great Skua's terrifying attacks. The bird approaches at head height, gathering speed, and pulling away at the last minute... well, almost. A clip on the head would be a mild punishment for the intruder.

Great Skuas often obtain food by robbing other seabirds, harrying them until they give up their catch. A gannet might be grabbed by the wing so that it loses balance and falls into the sea, where it will be attacked until it surrenders its fish.

Catharus minimus
Grey-cheeked Thrush

Catharos is the Greek word for 'pure', perhaps referring to the species' unadorned plumage. *Minimus* is the Latin word for 'least'.

This diminutive thrush breeds in North America and sometimes gets blown off course during migration to its winter quarters in Latin America. Almost invariably an appearance in Britain will occur on the Isles of Scilly, where strong south-west winds in late autumn will sometimes herald an arrival.

Check out the toes of *Certhia brachydactyla*, the Short-toed Treecreeper.

Cephalopterus glabricollis
Bare-necked Umbrellabird

The genus name comes from two Greek words. *Cephale* means 'head' and *opterux* means 'the best'.

The species name comes from two Latin words. *Glaber* means 'hairless' and *collis* means 'neck'.

This bird has an astonishing appearance. A little pendant hangs from the bare scarlet neck like an identity tag. The neck can enlarge when inflated during courtship or when showing aggression. An umbrella crest hangs over the male's forehead, while the female has a shorter crest more like a crew cut.

The Bare-necked Umbrellabird lives in Costa Rica and Panama. The author had a guide in Costa Rica who called the bird 'Elvis Presley' and gave every assurance that the bird would show up, but sadly that day there was no sighting. Elvis had left the room.

Certhia brachydactyla
Short-toed Treecreeper

Certhia comes from the Greek word *kerthios*, which was used by Aristotle to describe a small tree-dwelling bird.

Brakhus is the Greek word for 'short', and 'dactylos' is the Greek word for 'finger'. The toes are marginally shorter than those of *Certhia familiaris*, with which it shares very similar cryptic plumage.

– *C. familiaris*
Common Treecreeper

Familiaris is a Latin word meaning

An Inspiration for Composers?

Some people have wondered whether Beethoven's Symphony No.2 was inspired by the song of the Cetti's Warbler. The opening notes in the bird's song resemble the opening bars of the fourth movement. In his Symphony No.6 Beethoven appears to borrow from the repertoire of the Common Quail as the oboe seems to play 'wet my lips', while the clarinet calls out 'cuckoo', and the flute warbles away like a nightingale.

Was Beethoven's music influenced by our feathered friends?

Perhaps there is no conscious imitation here. The sounds of nature maybe lodged unwittingly in Beethoven's mind during long country walks. Our prairies and hills were alive with birdsong long before the arrival of humans. When we began to sing, perhaps we borrowed from the songs of nature, instead of starting from square one.

'familiar', or 'homely'. The treecreeper is the only small brown bird in Britain which habitually feeds by creeping mouse-like along tree-trunks. It is often seen with parties of foraging tits in the winter months.

Unlike the nuthatches, treecreepers cannot descend a tree head-first. These are tiny, frail birds which huddle together for warmth in a tree crevice during cold winter nights.

Cettia cetti
Cetti's Warbler

The bird is named after Francesco Cetti (1726–1778), a Catholic priest, mathematician and zoologist who collected specimens from Sardinia.

Charadrius alexandrinus
Kentish Plover

Charadrius comes from the Greek word *kharada*, meaning a 'ravine'.

The specific name is geographical and refers to the city in Egypt.

The bird no longer nests in Kent, or anywhere in Britain.

The Kentish Plover breeds on sandy coasts, but the tourist industry has done it no favours. Hotels, leisure centres, caravan sites, all of which satisfy our desire to be near water, have disturbed its peace.

Killdeer, *Charadrius vociferus*, in full voice.

– C. morinellus
Eurasian Dotterel

Morinellus comes from the Latin word *morio*, which means a 'fool' or 'jester'.

The English word Dotterel means an 'old fool', and refers to the ease with which the bird can be caught.

The male incubates and raises the young, while the female finds another male and lays another clutch. Maybe he is an old fool, yet he has the brains to feign injury when a predator or human approaches, dragging his wing to lure the intruder away from the eggs or young.

– C. vociferus
Killdeer

The specific name comes from the Latin *vox*, meaning 'voice', and *ferox*, meaning 'strong'.

Found across the Americas, the Killdeer is named onomatopoeically. Whether in flight or on the ground, the call is 'killdeer', much repeated. The nest is built on rough ground, and the spotted eggs are well disguised as stones.

The Killdeer could qualify for an Oscar, so realistic is its distraction display. Any intruder will be entertained by wing-dragging and wing-flapping, accompanied by the most pitiful of cries. When the predator or intruder has been lured to a safe distance, the Killdeer suddenly 'heals' and flies away.

Chelidoptera tenebrosa
Swallow-winged Puffbird

The genus name comes from *xelidon*, the Greek word for a 'swallow', and *pterux,* the Greek word for a 'wing'.

The specific name comes from *tenebrae*, a Latin word for 'darkness', and refers to the dark nesting site, which is well dug into a sandbank.

Also known as Swallow-wing, this species belongs to the family Bucconidae, from the Latin word, *bucco,* meaning 'clown'. Some family members (for example, the Spotted Puffbird, *Bucco tamatia*) have a colourful, clown-like appearance.

The English name puffbird refers to the loose and plentiful plumage and short tail, which gives the birds a 'puffed-out' appearance.

Chlidonias hybrida
Whiskered Tern

Chlidonias refers to a genus of birds known as 'marsh terns'. Its members are generally smaller than sea terns, much darker in colour, and favour freshwater marsh environments. *Chelidon* is the Greek word for a 'swallow', and *eidon* comes from the Greek word 'to see'. They look like

swallows with their buoyant flight.

Hibrida is the Latin for 'hybrid'. The ornithologist Pallas (1741–1811) thought the bird might be a hybrid of White-winged Black Tern and Common Tern.

– C. niger
Black Tern

Niger is the Latin word for 'black'.

The days have long since gone when Thomas Pennant (1726–1798), the English naturalist, writing in 1769, could talk of 'vast flocks of Black Terns, whose calls were deafening'. Extensive draining of the English fens wiped out the entire population by 1840. Marsh terns don't dive like sea terns, but pick food from the surface of the water.

Chroicocephalus ridibundus
Black-headed Gull

The genus name comes from two Greek words. *Khroizo* means 'to colour' and *cephale* means 'head'.

The species name comes from the Latin word *ridere*, meaning 'to laugh'. Confusingly, there is an American species called Laughing Gull (see *Leucophaeus atricilla*), which has a much more high-pitched cackle than the Black-headed Gull.

Gulls' eggs were a source of food for hundreds of years, and Leadenhall Market in London sold up to 300,000 every year, but the birds and their eggs are now protected by law. There are, however, a few licensed traders who can cull gulls

Whiskered Tern, *Chlidonias hybrida.*

and sell their eggs, at a hefty price.

A number of gull species have moved inland, so that the generic term 'seagull' hardly applies any longer. Black-headed Gulls are a familiar sight in a wide variety of habitats, and their airborne skills bring them quickly to 'flung' bread.

This lovely bird is one of a number of brightly coloured species introduced to Britain from Asia, in this case from China and Myanmar. The English name commemorates Countess Amherst (1762–1838), who brought specimens to Britain in 1828.

Chrysolophus amherstiae
Lady Amherst's Pheasant
Chrysolophus comes from two Greek words, meaning 'golden crest'.

– *C. pictus*
Golden Pheasant
The species name *pictus* comes from the Latin word for 'painted'.

A young child's imaginary *Chrysolophus* pheasant, by Maya, aged 8.
In reality the birds in this genus are more outlandish than the fictitious version.

The Golden Pheasant was introduced to Europe from China as a gamebird, but proved to be a sporting failure. When the males are alarmed they simply run through the woods instead of taking flight. In the air they would make a perfect target. The female is even less 'sporting'. She wisely squats down motionless when alarmed, and her drab plumage gives excellent camouflage.

Ciconia ciconia
White Stork

Ciconia is the Latin word for 'stork'. The word may come from *cicur*, meaning 'domesticated', as the birds frequently nest in close proximity to human dwellings. This is common in mainland Europe, and there is even a record of a pair nesting on St Giles High Kirk in Edinburgh in 1416. The large nest may be shared by other inhabitants – sparrows, starlings and jackdaws find a home there, as do feather mites and ticks.

Strangely, the droppings and faeces are often smeared on the legs. When these materials evaporate, the cooling effect is known as 'urohidrosis'. The word comes from the Greek: *ouron* for 'urine', *hydro* for 'water'.

Why is the bird associated with the delivery of babies? Who better than the stork, which has disappeared for several months to spend the winter on the African savannah, to return in the spring when new life begins.

Ciconia ciconia, White Stork, nesting on a building.

Cinclus cinclus
White-throated Dipper

Cinclus is the Latin word for 'apron' or 'girdle', and refers to the bird's white breast.

The dipper is a bird of fast-flowing streams, and can swim and 'fly' underwater. The diet is insect larvae and nymphs, and also small fish and fish eggs. The species was once persecuted in parts of Scotland, and bounties were paid, in the mistaken belief that they damaged fish stocks through the predation of salmon eggs and fry.

Circaetus gallicus
Short-toed Snake-Eagle

The genus name comes from *circus*, the Latin word for a 'circle', and *aetos*, the Greek word for an 'eagle'.

Gallicus is a geographical term, meaning 'Gaul'.

As the English name suggests, the diet is restricted to snakes and occasionally lizards, and the bird needs a healthy population of snakes in order to survive. Prey as large as the Montpellier Snake are spotted from around 500m (1,600ft) above the ground, as the bird circles

Cisticola juncidis, the Zitting Cisticola, giving its insect-like 'zitting' song.

on updraughts. These snakes can grow to 1.8m (6ft) in length, and bird and reptile can become enmeshed as they struggle together.

Circus cyaneus
Hen Harrier

Circus is a Latin word meaning 'circle' and makes reference to the bird's hunting technique, which involves continuously quartering the same ground, looking out for prey to devour.

Cyaneus comes from the Greek word for 'blue', after the blue-grey plumage of the adult male, which was often called the 'grey ghost' because of its spectral image.

The male is polygamous and will have up to five mates. The females incubate

the eggs and spend more time feeding the young than the male.

Hen Harriers often share the same habitat with Short-eared Owls, and the raptors will sometimes harry these birds and steal their prey.

– C. pygargus
Montagu's Harrier

The specific name comes from *puge*, the Greek word for 'rump', and *argos*, the Greek word for 'shining white'.

The English name renders homage to the naturalist George Montagu (1753–1815), whose *Ornithological Dictionary*, published in 1802, separated the Hen Harrier from similar-looking Montagu's Harrier.

Cisticola juncidis
Zitting Cisticola

The genus name comes from the Greek word *kisthios*, meaning the 'rock-rose'. *Colere* is the Latin word 'to dwell'.

The specific name comes from the Latin *iuncus*, meaning a 'reed'.

In courtship the male cisticola has a zigzag flight, calling continually with a 'zitting' song.

Clamator glandarius
Great Spotted Cuckoo

The genus name *clamato*r is the Latin word for a 'shouter'.

The species name comes from *glans*, the Latin word for 'acorn'.

This handsome bird is found from the Iberian Peninsula to the Middle East, and south to southern Africa. It is a brood parasite, often using members of the crow family such as magpies as hosts. The cuckoo chick, however, does not eject other young from the nest, although they often die of starvation as the cuckoo has the biggest appetite. Moreover the female cuckoo may lay several eggs in each nest. The young cuckoos produce a body secretion which deters predators such as raptors and cats.

Coccothraustes coccothraustes
Hawfinch

The Hawfinch has the longest binomial name of any European bird.

The scientific name comes from *kokkis*, which is the Greek word for 'seed', and *thrauw*, which is the Greek word for 'shatter'.

In the English name 'Haw' refers to the red berry of the hawthorn. The bill is huge and powerful, and can employ a force equivalent to a load of nearly 50kg (110lb) to crack open food items such as cherry stones.

Columba palumbus
Common Woodpigeon

Kolumbos was the ancient Greek for a 'diver', from the verb *kolumbao*, 'to dive headlong'. The verb is used by Aristophanes (c.446–386 BC), referring to the bird's swimming and plunging motions in the air. *Palumbus* was the Latin name for a 'pigeon'.

Aristophanes was a Greek playwright, whose words were often spoken by birds, frogs, and so on, making cryptic references to Athenian politics and society.

A Polyglot Family

It seems as if almost every vocal sound made by humans, in sickness or in health, has been given as a name to one of the cisticolas. There are birds whose specific names are Bubbling, Chirping, Churring, Croaking, Piping, Rattling, Siffling, Singing, Tinkling, Trilling, Wailing, Whistling, and finally, Winding Cisticola. These adjectives refer not to their health, but to their voices.

His play, *The Birds*, has 24 species of birds, among them the Hoopoe and Waxwing. The pigeon is identified with the Greek goddess Hera, goddess of marriage and fertility. There are modern adaptations of his plays.

In Victorian times, young woodpigeons were sometimes tied by the leg to the branches, so that they were unable to leave the nest. The adults continued to feed them. When they were considered fat enough for the pot, they were made into pigeon pie.

Members of the pigeon family have one strange behaviour shared by no other family of birds. Pigeons drink like horses. They suck the water through their mouths. Others fill the bill, tip it upwards, and gravity does the rest.

Coracias garrulus
European Roller

The genus name comes from the Latin word *corax,* meaning a 'raven', reflecting its superficial structural resemblence to members of the crow family. The plumage of the adults is a bright azure blue, and rollers feed by watching for prey from a perch, and diving for food items in the same way as a giant shrike.

The specific name is the Latin word for 'chattering' or 'talkative'. Rollers are noisy and aggressive at the nest, and intruders are intimidated by the rolling dives directed from overhead. The English name refers to the aerial acrobatics of the display flight.

Corvus corone
Carrion Crow

Corvus is the Latin for a 'raven', and *corone* is the Greek word for a 'crow'.

In Japan some Carrion Crows of the eastern subspecies *orientalis* (a geographical term) have developed a taste for walnuts. These delicacies are hard-shelled, so the crows have found an ingenious way of preparing their food – they get human beings to do the work for them. A walnut is placed on the road beside the traffic lights, when they show the colour red. The walnut is then retrieved after the cars have broken the hard shell. Winter tyres with a deep thread seem to work best!

– C. frugilegus
Rook

Frugilegus is the Latin for fruit-gatherer, from *frux*, meaning 'fruit', and *legere* 'to gather'.

The Rook is another member of this clever family. When kept in captivity they learn to use tools to get food. In one experiment a Rook was placed near a tub of water, with a worm floating on the surface, and some rocks nearby. The water level was too low for the bird to reach the worm, so the bird filled the tub with rocks until the water level was high enough.

Rook, *Corvus frugilegus*.

– C. monedula
Western Jackdaw

Monedula comes from the Latin word *moneta*, which means 'money'. This jackdaw has a habit of picking up shiny objects such as coins. The birds are clever and have been kept as pets. They can also be taught a few words, but this involves cutting the tongue to make it pliable. This habit seems to have died a happy death.

– C. moneduloides
New Caledonian Crow

The specific name comes from *monedula*, the 'jackdaw' in Latin, and *oides*, from the Greek verb 'to see'. The bird 'looks like' a jackdaw.

This is another clever crow – reputedly the most intelligent of all bird species – and it is capable of using a stick to winkle grubs from the hollows of trees.

The stick is not intended to spear or to stab the prey, but rather as an irritant. The grub of a beetle has small, sharp jaws which can inflict a painful bite when attacked. As the stick is prodded about, the grub reacts by clamping its jaws around the offending object. It is then hauled to the surface and eaten. Young crows will take about a year to master the technique.

Cotinga amabilis
Lovely Cotinga

The genus name comes from the Latin verb *tingere*, which means 'to stain' or 'to dye'. The plumage is a brilliant mix of lavender, purple and sky-blue. The pigment responsible for this glory is 'cotingin'. Cells in the cotinga's feathers have a series of tiny spores which are spaced in such a way that the colour blue is reflected back to our eyes. Yale University has attempted to produce the same effect, and the same intense colour, in laboratories.

Whatever the science, birdwatchers in Central America are spellbound at the sight of such loveliness. The specific name reflects their admiration. *Amabilis* is the Latin word for 'loveable' or 'lovely'.

Coturnix coturnix
Common Quail

Coturnix is the Latin word for 'quail'. Perhaps it comes from the word *cothurnus*, meaning 'tragedy', but this is uncertain. Yet there is a plaintive tone to the bird's call, transcribed as 'wet my lips, wet

The tiny Common Quail, *Coturnix coturnix*.

Quail: A Tasty Morsel

All species of quail are tiny birds, and they have long been a culinary favourite, even though an adult has barely enough meat to make a small starter.

Quail eggs are, as one would expect, miniscule, but they are eaten almost universally. In Japan they are often eaten raw, while in Europe they can be deep-fried or used as a topping on a hot dog. In Central America they are served as a beer accompaniment. The author recalls a visit to an open-air bar in Mexico where they were laid out like crisps or peanuts.

my lips'. The English name, quail, makes reference to the bird's secretive and timid nature, well hidden until it is disturbed, then setting off with a great flurry of wing-beats, never more than waist-high.

Cracticus tibicen
Australian Magpie

Cracticus is derived from the Greek *kraktos*, meaning 'noisy'.

The species name is from the Latin word *tibicen*, which means 'flute-player'.

The Australian Magpie is a great singer, covering a range of almost four octaves. The bird moves with ease through basso profundo to soprano, and can mimic

Cracticus tibicen, the Australian Magpie, is not closely related to magpies in the crow family.

Cuculus canorus, Common Cuckoo, in distinctive song.

the songs of at least 35 other bird species, as well as cats and dogs. Although the bird is not a 'corvid', and quite unrelated to the magpies in the crow family, it shares their intelligence. It has learned to flip over the Cane Toad, a highly poisonous creature, and eat the underparts. The magpie can also rub off the stings of wasps and bees before devouring them.

This species is aggressive when defending its territory, and pedestrians and cyclists need to be wary when a pair has young. Yet they are still loved enough to be the emblem of Melbourne's Collingwood Football Club, which has the nickname 'the magpies'.

Crex crex
Corncrake

The scientific name uses a literary device, onomatopoeia, and simply replicates the 'crex crex' call of the male in courtship. The bird is hard to find, even in short grass or stubble, as it can throw its voice in all directions.

Cuculus canorus
Common Cuckoo

Cuculus comes from the Middle English word for 'imitative' or 'repetitive'.

Canorus is the Latin word for 'tuneful'.

The common name is, of course, onomatopoeic.

The Common Cuckoo is a brood parasite, which means it lays its eggs in other birds' nests. It can then absolve itself from chick-raising duties and fly off to the sun before other migrant birds. By July the adults are well and truly absentee parents, enjoying the African weather while some tiny passerine wears itself out feeding the monster young. Its raptor-like shape encourages smaller birds to flee the nest, leaving the cuckoo free to exploit the structure as a host home for its own offspring.

'Cuckold' is a word used by Shakespeare for an adulterous wife.

Cursorius cursor
Cream-coloured Courser

Both parts of the scientific name come from the Latin word *currere*, meaning 'to run'. The sandy-coloured plumage of this bird acts as perfect camouflage in its desert habitat.

Cyanocitta cristata
Blue Jay

The genus name comes from two Greek words: *cyanos* means 'blue', and *kitta* means 'chattering'.

The Latin word *cristatus*, refers to the raised feathers on the head.

In captivity the Blue Jay can interact playfully with humans and has displayed evidence of tool-use, using folded paper to rake in food pellets from outside its cage. In the wild the bird's alarm call, consciously or otherwise, notifies smaller birds that a predator is nearby.

Cyanolanius madagascarinus
Madagascar Blue Vanga

The genus name comes from the Greek word *cyanos*, meaning 'blue'.

An intelligent and perhaps thoughtful Blue Jay, *Cyanocitta cristata*, illustrated in an 'art nouveau' style.

A Successful Twitch

When a rare bird appears in Britain, word spreads very quickly through social media. So when a Cream-coloured Courser appeared on a golf course in Kingston, Herefordshire, in 2012, around 2,000 birdwatchers appeared as if by magic.

This happened to be on the day when senior members played their monthly medal, but it was virtually impossible to play the eighth hole. Elderly gentlemen, weaving a path through cameras, tripods and birders with binoculars, simply gave up and returned 'no-score' on their cards. Thankfully it was all taken in good humour, the 19th hole did a roaring trade, and on a competition day everyone was a winner.

The species name is geographical.

Visitors to Madagascar will quickly add this dazzling bird to their list. When a large chunk of East Africa broke away some 70 million years ago, the formation of the archipelago resulted in high levels of endemism, not just among birds, but in most forms of life, not least Madagascar's magnificent lemurs!

Cyanopica cyanus
Azure-winged Magpie

The scientific name comes from the Greek word *cyanos*, which means 'blue'. The word is used twice, as if to underline the radiance of the bird's plumage.

These lovely birds are members of the crow family. It was formerly considered to be a species with two distinct populations separated by thousands of miles, with one in east Asia and the other in Iberia, although the latter has now been 'split' as a separate species, *Cyanopica cooki*, the Iberian Magpie.

In some fascinating studies, the question of 'altruism' has been studied in these birds. Do individual birds help each other at low or no cost to the donor? These magpies are seen to provide food to their group members spontaneously, without the recipient having to beg for food.

Cyanopsitta spixii
Spix's Macaw

The name comes from two Greek words. *Cyanos* means 'blue' and *Psittikos* means 'parrot'. Johann von Spix (1781–1826) was a German naturalist who collected a skin of this species in 1819.

This small and lovely macaw is now considered extinct in the wild. Deforestation through logging, burning and cattle grazing has taken a heavy toll on its habitat.

Recently Brazil has forbidden the export of its wildlife, which has driven the illicit bird-trade underground. However there are captive-breeding programmes for Spix's Macaw. Probably the largest is a private collection in Kuwait which houses a total of 64 birds, many of them hatched successfully in large aviaries. It is hoped that some birds may one day be returned to a suitable area of habitat in Brazil, whence they originated.

Cygnus bewickii
Bewick's Swan

Cygnus is a Latin word for 'swan'.

The species name pays tribute to naturalist and illustrator Thomas Bewick (1753–1828). His two-volume work, *A History of British Birds*, was to set the standard of identification books for some time. Each bird is identified by its binomial name, with a woodcut illustration, then a short description, and finally a 'tailpiece'. The tailpiece was a small woodcut showing examples of village life. In one of these a woman is putting out her washing, when a chicken makes muddy footprints on a shirt which has fallen off the clothes line. In another a

'Swan swan', better known as *Cygnus olor* or the Mute Swan.

man is hiding behind a hedge, and shoots a snipe, which tumbles out of the air. In yet another there is a thirsty traveller, drinking water from his own hat. The tailpiece had little to do with ornithology, but much to do with his gentle humour.

The Bewick's is the smallest of the Old World swans, breeding in Siberia and wintering in Western Europe.

– C. olor
Mute Swan

Olor is another Latin word for 'swan', so the scientific name translates as 'swan swan'.

These birds make grunting, snorting and hissing noises, but the most memorable is the 'throbbing' sound of the wings, which can be audible from a mile away.

The phrase 'swan song' refers to the legend that the bird sings a haunting lament at the time of its death.

The Roman poet, Ovid, reported that the swan sings her own funeral song and Ancient Greek writers Plato and Aristotle both refer to the legend.

Cypseloides senex
Great Dusky Swift

The genus name comes from the Greek word *kupsely*, meaning a 'hollow vessel', with the derivative *kupselis*, meaning 'the nest of a swallow or martin'. *Oides* is a form of the past tense of the Greek verb *horaw*, meaning 'to see'. A good translation would be 'looks like'.

The species name comes from the Latin word *senex* which means an 'old man'. The greyish head does have an aged look.

The author watched in disbelief as these birds went crashing through the waterfalls at Iguazú, a site where the film *The Mission* was shot. The Iguazú falls can be reached from the Brazilian or the

Argentinian side, and such is the spectacle, with water tumbling from a height of 82m (270ft), that two international airports are needed to serve the visitors.

Great Dusky Swifts are among the larger members of their family, with bullet-shaped bodies that fly through

the air at great speed. They are able to hurtle behind the cataracts to rest and breed on the vertical cliffs behind. Not bad for an 'old man'.

Great Dusky Swifts, *Cypseloides senex*, nest behind the torrents of water at the world-famous Iguazú Falls, on the border of Brazil and Argentina.

Plenty of mirth at the billabong with the Laughing Kookaburra, *Dacelo novaeguineae*.

Dacelo novaeguineae
Laughing Kookaburra

The genus name is an anagram of *alcedo*, the Latin word for a 'kingfisher'. Kookaburras are the largest of all the kingfishers.

The species name is a geographical term, as the bird is native to Australia and New Guinea

Young kookaburras take part in family chores for several years after fledging, including protecting the territory, collecting food for new chicks, and even taking their turn to incubate the eggs. The cackling call of one kookaburra is an invitation for several to join together in a chorus of manic laughter.

Daption capense
Cape Petrel

The genus name comes from *daption*, the Greek word for a 'little devourer', or a 'hungry child'.

The species name refers to the Cape of Good Hope in South Africa, where it was first collected.

The English name 'petrel' makes reference to Saint Peter, who walks on the water in the gospel narratives. The bird is also known as the 'Cape Pigeon', as it pecks at food on the water like a pigeon or a hungry child (*daption*). Another name, the 'Pintado Petrel', uses the Spanish word for 'painted'.

This is a bird of the southern oceans,

Daption capense, Cape Petrel, on the wing.

which will follow ships for scraps and carcasses thrown overboard. This forms a toxic mix in the bird's stomach, which it will spit out when threatened. The stench is very hard to eradicate.

Delichon urbicum
House Martin

The Greek word *delichon* is an anagram of *chelidon*, and means 'swallow'.

Urbs is the Latin word for 'city'.

During construction of the mud nest House Sparrows will frequently attempt to steal the space, but once the nest is completed, the entrance is too small for them. There are studies which show that wandering males will copulate briefly with an already mated female, so that her egg clutch will include a 'bastard' egg. As if to guard against such extra-pair copulations, male House Martins seem to follow the female as if to keep a watchful eye, to avoid being 'cuckolded'.

Dendrocygna viduata
White-faced Whistling-Duck

The genus name comes from the Greek word *dendron*, meaning 'tree', and the Latin word *cygnus*, meaning 'swan'.

The species name comes from the Latin word *vidua*, meaning 'widow'. The white face suggests a widow in mourning.

The voice is full of brio. The sight of a thousand birds arriving at dawn, with their lovely three-note whistles, makes a cheerful start to any birder's day.

Delichon urbicum, the House Martin, gathering mud for nest-building.

Dicrurus adsimilis
Fork-tailed Drongo

The genus name comes from the Latin word *Dicrotus*, which means a 'double-oared vessel' and refers to the forked tail.

Adsimilis is the Latin word for 'similar'.

This drongo is an African species which has developed a devious method of acquiring food with very little effort. The secret is in the tone of voice. When another bird or animal has found food to its liking, the drongo simply gives its alarm call, or mimics the alarm call of another species, and the victims flee terrified while the drongo helps itself to the leftovers. Meerkats and Pied Babblers are common targets.

The Wandering Albatross, *Diomedea exulans*, showing off its huge wingspan.

Diomedea exulans
Wandering Albatross

The word *Diomeda* makes reference to Diomedes, the Greek warrior in Homer's *The Iliad*. During the siege of Troy Diomedes enters the city inside a wooden horse. Allegedly a gift from the Greeks, the horse opens and Greek warriors leap fully armed from within. The memorable phrase, *Timeo Graecos et dona ferentes* (I fear the Greeks, even when they bring gifts), is used to describe an act of subterfuge. At the end of his life, on the island of Diomedea, there is a legend that the albatrosses sang the funeral song of Diomedes. In another legend the goddess Venus feels pity for his weeping companions and turns them into albatrosses, while in a different legend

Diomedes himself is transformed into an albatross at the end of his life.

Add to these stories the 'Rime of the Ancient Mariner', and little wonder that the albatross has been called the 'most legendary of all birds'. In Coleridge's poem, the sailor who killed the albatross is punished by having to wander the world aimlessly and eternally. In folklore, albatrosses were once thought of as the souls of lost sailors. The albatross is a long-lived bird, and one wonders which was the oldest, the bird or the mariner.

The specific name comes from *exult*, the Latin word for a 'wanderer', referring to its extensive flights around the southern oceans. The Wandering Albatross has the largest wingspan of any bird.

Dolichonyx oryzivorus
Bobolink

Dolichonyx comes from two Greek words: *dolichos* means 'long', and *onyx* means 'claw'.

The specific name comes from *oryza,* the Latin for 'rice', and *'vorare'*, the Latin for 'eat'.

The Bobolink was also known as the 'rice bird'. The migration route, from North America to Latin America, takes many birds through Jamaica, where they are called the 'butterbird'. There they were once eaten as a delicacy, having fattened up on rice.

Dromaius novaehollandiae
Emu

The genus name comes from the Latin word *dromas*, which means 'dromedary' or 'racer'. The species name is geographical

Some Notes on a National Treasure

In courtship it is the female Emu who makes the moves, while the male does the incubating. During incubation he will live on stored body fat and lose 30 per cent of his body weight as he doesn't eat or drink until the chicks are due to hatch. The female may desert the nest site completely and look for other males. She may produce three clutches of eggs in a season.

While some birds are foul-tasting, Emu meat is considered to be as succulent as the best beef. The extinction of the Kangaroo Island Emu was related to the chef's success at the dining table.

The long legs and humped back of the Emu, *Dromaius novaehollandiae*, are both reminiscent of a dromedary.

The sparrow-sized Lesser Spotted Woodpecker, *Dryobates minor*.

and means 'New Holland', which was an original name for Australia.

The flightless Emu is the largest bird in Australia, growing to a height of 1.7m (5.5ft), and able to sprint at 50kph (30mph). It is an important cultural symbol, appearing on coats of arms and featuring on stamps and coins.

Dromas ardeola
Crab-plover

Dromas is the Latin word for 'dromedary'. This is a bird of the Middle East, where camels are an integral part of life, and the Indian Ocean islands.

The specific name comes from *arduus,* the Latin word for 'lofty'.

The Crab-plover, as the name suggests, feeds mainly on crabs, and has some very odd characteristics. It can run quickly, and is a good swimmer. Flocks fly in 'V' formation like geese. They forage for food around the clock as diurnal, crepuscular and nocturnal feeders.

Crab-plovers nest in burrows and the constant temperature inside means they can leave the eggs or young unattended for two or three days. The newly hatched chicks, despite being feathered at birth, cannot walk for the first week or so and are fed 'on site'. Even after they leave the nest, the young cannot feed themselves and require a long period of parental care. Not surprisingly the Crab-plover has the genus *Dromas* all to itself.

Dumetella carolinensis, the Grey Catbird, is named after its cat-like calls.

Dryobates minor
Lesser Spotted Woodpecker

Druos is the Greek word for 'tree', and *bates* is the Greek word for 'walker'.

The Latin word *minor* means 'smaller'.

This tiny woodpecker can be hard to see as it favours the tops of trees, and can work its way along very small branches. Moreover the small nest-hole can be as high as 12m (40ft) above the ground. Early spring is the best time to find this woodpecker, when the trees are bare and the birds are active.

Dumetella carolinensis
Grey Catbird

The etymology of this American bird comes from the Latin *dumus*, meaning a 'thorny bush', while the last two syllables *ella* give it a diminutive form. This is literally the 'little bird of the thorn bushes'.

The French ornithologist Louis Vieillot (1748–1830) called it the *felivox*, Latin for cat (*felix*) and voice *(vox)*.

But like other members of the mimidae (literally 'mimics'), such as the mockingbirds, the catbird has a wide repertoire: it gives cat calls especially when threatened, but will also mimic tree frogs and other bird songs. With the explosion in digital technology mechanical sounds have been added. More often seen than heard, a thorny bush can sound like a mobile phone.

Ectopistes migratorius
Passenger Pigeon
The genus name is a Greek word meaning 'wandering' or 'moving about'.

The species name is a Latin word referring to its migratory habits.

How the Passenger Pigeon,
Ectopistes migratorius, met its fate.

The Extermination of America's Most Numerous Bird

In 1800 Passenger Pigeons numbered in the billions. As they migrated from northern North America to Mexico and the southern United States, a single flock might contain over one million birds. Their wing-beats could be heard from some distance, and their numbers literally darkened the sky. They nested in densely packed colonies and trees were bent under their weight. This was 'prodigal nature' on a huge scale.

Shooting parties competed for the number they killed. This was not target practice and it required no skill. Any gun pointed into the general direction of a flock would bag several birds. There were massacres on a grand scale, and trees were cut down with hundreds of young birds taken for the cooking pot.

Soon the bird was seldom seen. A few lingered in aviaries, and a prize of 1,500 US Dollars was offered to anyone who could find an active nest. But any effort was in vain. Within 100 years only, the most numerous bird in North America, considered to have a population of 3–5 billion, was extinct. The last of the species died in 1914 in the zoo at Cincinatti.

In 1911 the behavioural scientist Wallace Craig reckoned that the loud and strident and unmusical notes he heard were due to the huge colonies in which they nested, where each bird competed to be heard.

Elanus caeruleus
Black-winged Kite

The genus name comes from the Latin verb *lanio*, which means 'to tear to pieces'. The Latin noun *lanionius* makes reference to a 'butcher'.

Caeruleus is the Latin word for 'blue'.

These are birds of Africa and Asia, with a European foothold in the Iberian Peninsula. The Black-winged Kite lacks the forked tail of kites in the genus *Milvus*. They are usually seen hovering like a kestrel over open grassland, though in Africa they hunt by the roadside and are often killed by cars. Typically these birds will be seen gliding on wings held in a V-shape.

Emberiza citrinella
Yellowhammer

The genus name comes from an Old German word meaning 'bunting'.

Citrinella is a diminutive form in Italian, meaning a 'small yellow bird'.

The song has been transcribed as 'A little bit of bread and no cheese',

Emberiza citrinella, the Yellowhammer, in full song.

but because the birds learn the song from their fathers there are regional variations. Females will tend to mate with accents they hear as familiar, and will choose males with the largest musical repertoire.

This Eurasian species has been successfully introduced on the other side of the world in New Zealand.

– E. hortulana
Ortolan Bunting

The species name comes from the Latin word *hortulus*, which means a 'little garden'.

A Gourmet's Delight

For centuries French gourmets captured these tiny birds in nets on their migration to Africa, and kept them in cages where they were fed on millet until they doubled their weight. They were then drowned in armagnac, and roasted whole with spices and garlic. The diner sat with a towel over his head to retain the aroma. Some cynics said it was to hide from God! After all, the practice of using a towel was started by a priest. Perhaps he forgot that there was, indeed, nowhere to hide? The killing and cooking of Ortolan Buntings is now banned throughout the European Union.

The Christmas Card Bird

We have affection for the robin because it seems to love us. It approaches when we lay out our barbecue, perches on the gardener's spade watching hopefully as the earth is overturned, and may even enter the house with all the familiarity of a near relative. The purpose of this intimacy is food. But a robin's life is typically over in two or three years, so the bird that grew up with us yesterday is soon replaced by the next generation.

There is a dark side to our favourite Christmas card bird. The robin is a notorious bully, and will defend its patch with some ferocity. The male will sing throughout the winter, signalling that he alone has the title deeds to the garden.

European Robin, *Erithacus rubecula*.

Eremophila alpestris
Horned Lark

The genus name comes from the Greek word *eremites*, meaning 'living in the desert'. *Eremos* is the Greek word for lonely and gives us the word hermit. The latter part of the genus name comes from *filia*, a Greek word suggesting 'a love of'.

The specific name is a Latin word meaning 'of the mountains'. *Alpes* is the Latin word for the Alps.

In Britain the bird is seen as a winter visitor along our coastlines, where it is called the Shore Lark.

Erithacus rubecula
European Robin

Erithacus is a word from Ancient Greek, referring to an unknown bird, probably the robin. *Rubecula* comes from *ruber*, the Latin for 'red'. *Rubescere* is the Latin verb meaning to blush. The robin's bright colour extends well up onto its face.

Clown of the birdtable? The Red-headed Barbet, *Eubucco bourcierii*.

Eubucco bourcierii
Red-headed Barbet

The genus term comes from the Greek prefix *eu* meaning 'well' or 'good', and *bucco*, the Latin word for a 'clown'. The bird is spectacularly coloured, with a brilliant red head, which does give it a 'clownish' appearance. Some of the lodges in Costa Rica and Panama advertise themselves on the certainty of the Red-headed Barbet appearing on the bird table.

Jules Bourcier (1797–1873), who is honoured in the species name, was a French naturalist who was French Consul to Ecuador from 1849–1850 and became an expert on hummingbirds, two of which are named after him.

The barbet family number around 60, and are so called because of the bristles on the base of their stout bills. The word resonates with 'barber', and the bristles may be abundant, or almost missing.

The birds call loudly and pairs may duet. Birders sometimes place them in a special, completely non-scientific category – 'brain-fever birds' – birds from a variety of families which can madden us with their loud repetitive calls.

Eudyptes chrysolophus
Macaroni Penguin

The etymology is entirely Greek. *Eu* means 'good' and *dyptes* is a 'diver'. *Chrise* means 'golden' and *lophos* means 'head'.

The English adjective comes from macaronism, a term descriptive of a

dress style with excessive ornamentation, part of which might be a hat with yellow feathers. The line in the song 'Yankee Doodle', 'Stuck a feather in his hat and called it macaroni', refers to the same fashion style. It's hard to look at a penguin and feel angry!

Euphonia luteicapilla
Yellow-crowned Euphonia

The genus name comes from *eu,* a Greek prefix meaning 'well' and *phony,* a Greek word meaning 'voice'.

The species name comes from *luteus,* a Latin word for 'yellow', and *caput,* the Latin word for 'head'.

These are tiny songsters of the finch family, inhabiting Neotropical regions.

Northern Red Bishop, *Euplectes orix.*

Euplectes orix
Northern Red Bishop

The genus term comes from two Greek words: *eu* is a prefix meaning 'well' or 'good', and *plectes* comes from the word 'plaited' or 'groomed'.

The species name comes from a Latin word *ori-chalcum,* meaning 'yellow-copper'.

The English name is based on the colour worn by a bishop.

Macaroni Penguin, *Eudyptes chrysolophus,* with 'feathers in their hats'.

Falco concolor
Sooty Falcon

Falco comes from the Latin word for a sickle (*falx*) and makes reference to the bird's silhouette in flight.

The specific name is the Latin word for 'unicoloured', referring to the uniform grey plumage. There are two colour morphs, sooty grey and nearly black.

– F. eleonorae
Eleonora's Falcon

The species name commemorates Eleanor of Arborea (1347–1404), a Sardinian Judge whose 'Carta de Logu' (Body of Laws) was published in 1395 and legalised the protection of nesting falcons.

Peregrine Falcon, *Falco peregrinus* – the world's fastest bird.

– F. peregrinus
Peregrine Falcon

Peregrinus is the Latin for 'traveller', and fits in well as the bird is found in every continent.

Some outrageous claims have been made about the speed attained by the bird as it stoops from a height to strike its prey. 600mph (965kph) has been suggested, but at that speed we would surely hear the bird equivalent of a sonic boom. Using modern techniques of measurement we can safely say the Peregrine can achieve 200mph (320kph) in its stoop.

In the 1950s and 1960s Peregrine populations dropped alarmingly. The culprit was DDT. Farmers sprayed it on their crops, and it entered the digestive tracts of the falcons. Its use is now banned and Peregrine numbers have increased.

– *F. rusticolus*
Gyr Falcon

The species name originates from *rusticulus*, a Latin word meaning 'countryman'.

The English name 'Gyr', probably comes from the Latin word *gyrus*, meaning a 'circle' and makes reference to the bird's movement in search of prey.

The Gyr Falcon has a long association with humans in the art of falconry, but due to its rarity was the preserve of noblemen and royalty. Rarely would a man of lesser rank be seen with a Gyr Falcon. In 12th century China, they were commonly used to hunt swans. Today, in the Middle East, they sell for huge sums of money, used by falconers hunting desert birds, especially Houbara Bustards.

Gyr Falcon belongs to a subgenus *Hierofalco*, along with the closely related Lanner, Saker and Lagger Falcons. The Greek *hieros* means 'sacred' and the Gyr Falcon is often depicted in heraldry with a cross above its head, making reference to Christ and the faith which believes in his mastery over the elements. In Ancient Egypt the god Horus is transformed as a falcon and becomes a letter in Egyptian hieroglyphics.

– *F. subbuteo*
Eurasian Hobby

The species name comes from *sub*, the Latin word for 'under' or 'lesser', and *buteo*, the Latin word for a 'buzzard'. As the etymology suggests, the hobby is a small falcon, whose slim build gives great agility in flight. The genus name is particularly apposite here (falcon comes from *falx*, the Latin word for a 'sickle'), as the long sickle-shaped wings enable the hobby to capture swifts in flight. Martins and swallows have a special alarm call when a hobby is sighted.

Falculea palliata
Sickle-billed Vanga

The genus name comes from the Latin word *falcarius*, meaning a 'sickle-maker'.

The species name is derived from the Latin verb *palleo*, which means to be 'pale'.

The First Super-lister

A member of the vanga family was the last bird sought by Phoebe Snetsinger as she travelled the world amassing a list containing the largest number of bird species seen by one person at that time. Sadly she died in Madagascar on 23rd November 1999, in a road traffic accident while in search of the Helmet Vanga. During her life she had seen a total of 8,398 species. Phoebe had been given a year to live after a cancer diagnosis, and decided to spend that time on bird expeditions. Happily she exceeded that prognosis by 20 years. She used to say her interest in birds 'began with a death sentence'.

Vanga was the Malagasy word for the Sickle-billed Vanga.

The vanga family is endemic to Madagascar, and is a good example of adaptive radiation, with the founding population diversifying to fill various niches in the 50 million years since separation from the African mainland. The Sickle-billed Vanga occupies the niche usually inhabited by woodpeckers, of which there are none in Madagascar. The long bill probes deep into tree holes, levering off the bark to get to the concealed prey.

Atlantic Puffin, *Fratercula arctica*.

Ficedula hypoleuca
Pied Flycatcher

The genus name comes from Latin: *ficus*, meaning a 'fig', *erede* meaning 'to eat', and *ula* , which gives the word a diminutive form. The family name means, literally, the 'small, fig-eating bird'.

The species name refers to the colour of the plumage: *Hypo* is a Greek word meaning 'below', and *leuco* is the Greek word for 'white'.

Fratercula arctica
Atlantic Puffin

The genus name is the diminutive form of the Latin word, *frater*, which means 'brother' or 'monk'. The black and white plumage of the Puffin resembles the monastic robes of a friar.

Arctica is geographical and refers to the 'Arctic'.

The English name refers to the 'puffed out' appearance of young birds which have been salted and dried for consumption. The fatty salted meat appears swollen. In Iceland the Puffin features on hotel menus, and the fresh heart of the bird is eaten raw as a delicacy.

This is a bird of northern Atlantic waters. It spends the winter at sea, when the bill fades to a dull grey rather than the bright colours of spring and summer. The 'sea parrot' is a common colloquial name.

Pied Flycatcher, *Ficedula hypoleuca*.

Fringilla coelebs
Common Chaffinch

The genus name comes from *fringillus*, the Latin word for a 'finch' or 'sparrow'.

A pair of Chaffinches, Fringilla coelebs.

– F. montifringilla
Brambling

The species name comes from two Latin words. *Mons* is the word for 'mountain', and *fringilla* is the word for 'finch'

The species name is the Latin word for 'celibate'. The male is often seen in the winter as solitary, or separate from the females, and therefore the word fits well. Linnaeus remarked that during the Swedish winter only the females migrated south to Italy.

Pairs do not mate for life, so come summer, as they build a lovely feather-lined nest with a new spouse, they forget their winter solitude.

The Brambling is a finch of northern Europe and Asia, and is wholly migratory. Thousands of birds can make up a single flock, and are often found in forests with beech–mast. As they fly from the forest floor, the white rump is a good identification feature. Although the diet is varied, beech–mast is a preferred option, perhaps to avoid competition with the chaffinch.

A Lost Way of Life

Writing in 1804, after a visit to St Kilda, Thomas Bewick, the author of *A History of British Birds*, wrote that 'No bird is of such use to the islanders as this. The fulmar supplies them with oil for their lamps, down for their beds, a delicacy for their tables, a balm for their wounds, and a medicine for their distempers'.

In mid-August thousands of young fulmars were harvested before they could fly. Men were lowered down the cliff-face by rope, and killed young birds by twisting their necks. Birds were preserved in barrels of salt, and their oil was stored in little pouches made from the stomachs of gannets. The oil was rich in vitamins A and D, and sold for five shillings per pint. The birds' feathers fetched a good price at 10 shillings per stone in weight.

After the harvesting of fulmar chicks, it was the turn of the gannets to be slaughtered. These were taken from the cliffs at night. The sentry bird was strangled, and then the killing began. As with the fulmar, its oil was stored and sold, as were the feathers, and the bird was considered a delicacy.

Then in 1930, when most residents were elderly, the island of St Kilda was evacuated, and a unique way of life, whose economy was based largely on two species of birds, was lost to modernity.

Fulmarus glacialis
Northern Fulmar

The genus name comes from Old Norse: *full* means 'foul', and *mar* means 'gull'. The word refers to the foul smell of their stomach oil. The bird's diet is fish, crustaceans and offal.

Glacialis is the Latin word for 'icy'.

The species' British range exploded in the 19th and 20th centuries, due partly to the availability of offal from the commercial fishing fleets. It is now found all around our coasts, whereas formerly it bred only St Kilda, a remote island off the west coast of Scotland.

Northern Fulmar, *Fulmarus glacialis*.

A Rufous Hornero, *Furnarius rufus*, stands guard at its oven-shaped nest.

Furnarius rufus
Rufous Hornero

The genus name comes from the Latin word *furnus*, which means 'oven'.

Rufus is the Latin word for 'red', and refers to the reddish–brown body and rusty coloured tail.

Horno is the Spanish word for 'oven'. As the name suggests, the hornero is a member of the ovenbird family and the nest is typical, being a large oven-like structure made of clay or dung, sometimes mixed with straw.

This species adjusts well to habitats modified by humans, such as parks and city suburbs, where they can be seen walking confidently on the ground. The Rufous Hornero is the national bird of Argentina.

Galerida theklae
Thekla Lark

The genus name comes from *galeritus,* a Latin adjective which means 'wearing a hat', and makes reference to the bird's crest.

The species name was given by the naturalist Alfred Brehm (1829–1884) to honour his sister Thekla Brehm, who died in 1857. Thekla is a common girl's name, and has a Greek etymology: *theos* is the word for 'God', and *kleios* is a word for 'glory'.

The Thekla Lark is common in North Africa and the Iberian Peninsula.

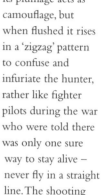

Thekla Lark, *Galerida theklae*, 'wearing a hat'.

It is distinguished from the very similar-looking Crested Lark chiefly by its song, which is more mimetic and often uttered from a perch.

Gallinago gallinago
Common Snipe

The genus and specific name both come from the New Latin, based on *gallina,* meaning 'little hen'.

The snipe has the longest bill of any British or European bird in proportion to its size, with nerve endings extending almost to the tip, making the bill a delicate organ of sensation. Worms and crustaceans, although completely out of sight, can be detected and identified below the surface.

While other waders such as Dunlins gather together in large numbers, the snipe favours life as a solitary feeder in a marshy puddle all by itself, like an infant at a party who can't join in the fun.

The snipe stays well hidden and its plumage acts as camouflage, but when flushed it rises in a 'zigzag' pattern to confuse and infuriate the hunter, rather like fighter pilots during the war who were told there was only one sure way to stay alive – never fly in a straight line. The shooting of pheasants, woodcock and grouse, by contrast, requires little skill. The word 'sniper' refers to a particularly skilled marksman.

During courtship the bird flies high before it plummets to the ground, producing a drumming sound by vibrating its tail feathers.

Gallinula chloropus
Common Moorhen

The genus name is the diminutive form of *gallina,* the Latin word for a hen.

The species name comes from *chloros,* the Greek word for 'green', and *pous,* the Greek word for a 'foot'.

Although not as gaudily plumed as its cartoon namesake, the Greater Roadrunner, *Geococcyx californianus* , is nevertheless a striking bird.

The English name uses the old meaning of *moor* as 'marsh', a word which perfectly describes its habitat.

Geococcyx californianus
Greater Roadrunner

The genus name comes from two Greek words: *Geo* is from the word for 'earth'. *Coccyx* means 'imitation', and gives us the words 'cuckoo' and 'cuckold'.

The specific name refers to its location. In other words, this is the 'ground–dwelling cuckoo from the Americas'. With its short wings it is not a strong flier and prefers to run from predators and chase after prey using its long legs. The roadrunner is able to kill small rattlesnakes, scorpions and black widow spiders by repeatedly banging them on the ground.

Geospiza difficilis
Sharp-beaked Ground-Finch

The genus name comes from *gy*, the Greek word for 'ground', and *spissus*, a Latin adjective meaning 'dispersed' or 'spread around'.

The species name is a Latin adjective meaning 'difficult' or 'troublesome'.

An alternative English name for this species is Vampire Finch. Typically finches eat seeds and invertebrates, and require water like other bird species.

It seems that at some point in the

past, the ancestors of these ground-finches were rummaging through the feathers of Red-footed and Blue-footed Boobies, picking off insects and parasites, when the skin on these birds began to break and the blood started to flow. The birds subsequently developed a taste for blood as a regular part of their diet.

Over time the bills of these finches have become longer and more pointed, to enable the birds to break through the skin more easily and indulge their ghoulish habits. The boobies sit quite unperturbed by this blood-letting.

There is a further descent into depravity. The finches also steal eggs as big as themselves. Unable to crack them open, the eggs are rolled against rocks until they shatter, so that the finches can consume the contents.

Vampire Finches, *Geospiza difficilis*, taking a drink of blood.

The Northern Bald Ibis, *Geronticus eremita*, is one of the world's rarest birds.

Geronticus eremita
Northern Bald Ibis

Geron was the Greek word for an 'old man'.

Eremita was the Greek word for a 'hermit'. Hermits and holy men would seek seclusion from the world's distractions by living in remote caves, often high in rocky mountains, in the same habitat as the ibis. In their loneliness, hermit monks would often have a bird or animal companion, perhaps a raven or dog. There is no record of the bald ibis being chosen to take away the solitude.

It was a Swiss doctor, Conrad Gessner (1516–1565), who first described the Northern Bald Ibis as a bird with a naked face, which looked like a hen and lived in the mountains. But the good doctor had already included, in his writings, a description of the unicorn! He named this new bird the 'forest raven' and his contemporaries must have wondered whether this was another flight of fancy.

Much later, birds fitting this

Dancing Red-crowned Cranes, *Grus japonensis*.

description were found in the Middle East and North Africa, and fossil evidence was found much closer to home, in Switzerland and other European countries. There are now reintroduction projects in Austria and Spain.

The Northern Bald Ibis is no beauty. Part of its appeal is its spectacular ugliness. Young children at a zoo will spend more time at this enclosure than at the cages holding the brightly coloured ornamental pheasants.

Glareola pratincola
Collared Pratincole

The genus name comes from *glarea*, the Latin word for 'gravel', which is a typical nesting habitat.

The species name comes from *pratum*, the Latin word for 'meadow', and *incola*, the Latin word for an 'inhabitant'.

Pratincoles hunt insect prey on the wing, rather like swallows.

Grus japonensis
Red-crowned Crane

Grus is the Latin word for 'crane', and *japonensis* is a geographical term meaning 'from Japan'. These are birds of serpentine beauty, with a stunning and elaborate courtship. The birds circle each other, bowing and raising their heads, calling and leaping into the air.

During the time of the shoguns, when only royals could carry guns, the birds were relatively safe, but once the restrictions were lifted the slaughter began. Hunters went on a shooting-fest, to provide feathers to adorn hats and other accessories. By the end of the 19th century the species was thought to be absent from Japan. Then a tiny population was found in northern Hokkaido and the government moved in to provide protection. Local schoolchildren thought that the birds laboured hard to feed when the ground was frozen, and began to scatter corn on the ground. That tradition continues to this day.

In Japan brides wear images of the crane on their dresses. The bird was culturally associated with a long life, as brides would hope for a long marriage. Perhaps a toast to the crane would be fitting: *Ad multos annos vives, plurimosque annos vives.* 'May you live for many years, and for many more years after that'.

Gymnogyps californianus
California Condor

The genus name comes from two Greek words. *Gymnos*, means 'naked', and refers to the bare head, and *gyps* means 'vulture'. The species name is geographical.

These are the largest flying birds in North America, with a wingspan of 3m (10ft), and the ability to soar at altitudes of 4,500m (15,000ft). The California Condor is a scavenger, and when the prey is large, a group of birds may gorge themselves and be unable to fly for several hours.

These birds are perhaps best known as the subjects of a captive-breeding programme. When the population in the wild dropped to just 10 birds, these were taken into captivity. Now there are well

California Condor, *Gymnogyps californianus*, from the reintroduction scheme – note the wing-tags.

over 260 birds in the wild, but mortality is high as they succumb to death on powerlines. Before release into the wild, young condors are now trained to avoid electricity cables.

This aversion-conditioning programme has resulted in fewer deaths. The main cause of mortality is now death through lead poisoning, as birds eat carcasses shot by humans. They clearly fare better where human populations have low density.

Gypaetus barbatus
Lammergeier

The genus name comes from two Greek words: *Gyps* means 'vulture', and *aetos* means 'eagle'. *Barbatus* is a Latin word meaning 'bearded'.

Lammergeier is a German word for a 'killer of lambs'.

The Lammergeier, which is also known as the Bearded Vulture, has an omnivorous diet. Household waste is eaten, as well as excrement, insects, eggs and other birds. As human waste-disposal methods have improved, its ability to scavenge has decreased.

Its favoured food is the marrow from bones. Bones can be dropped from a great height to shatter on the ground below and expose the marrow. An old name for the bird, Ossifrage, comes from two Latin words. *Os* is the word for 'bone', and *frangere* is the verb 'to break'. The bird prefers habitats where predators such as wolves and eagles hunt successfully, and leave the bones of a meal behind.

Gelada Gymnastics

The author watched Lammergeiers in Ethiopia in spring 2006 – a group of four vultures hunting beside the monastery of Debre Libanos, which was built by

emperor Haile Selassie. They had perhaps gathered at a kill, as a bone came tumbling to earth. Amazingly, as the birds flew low over the escarpment, Gelada monkeys leapt into the air in an effort to catch them. This piece of play-acting has probably been played out for centuries. The birds are quite safe, as they veer away at the last minute, but for the Gelada perhaps hope springs eternal.

Strange goings on at the monastery.

A Lammergeier at a kill will shun the meat in favour of the bone marrow.

Gyps bengalensis
White-rumped Vulture

The word *Gyps* resonates with the words 'Egypt' and 'gypsy'.

The species name is geographical, with bird's range centred on the Indian Subcontinent, where this species, along with two others, formerly occurred in such numbers as to darken the skies. Since about 1990 the subcontinent has lost an estimated 35 million vultures (see boxed text).

– G. fulvus
Griffon Vulture

Fulvus is a Latin word for 'greyish'.

The Griffon was a mythical creature with the head of an eagle and the body of a lion.

– G. rueppellii
Rüppell's Vulture

The species name makes reference to the German naturalist Edouard Rüppell (1794–1881), who was the first naturalist to traverse Ethiopia, collecting skins along the way. This bird is considered to be the highest flyer of them all, recorded at a height of 11,300m (37,100ft), which is 2,450m (8,040ft) higher than the summit of Everest.

The Problem with Diclofenac

Vultures are nature's scavengers, cleaning up rotting animal carcasses. But in the Indian Subcontinent their numbers have plummeted. As many as 40 million birds have died, mostly in Bangladesh. In their absence, they have been replaced by feral dogs, jackals and rats. The incidence of rabies has increased. If there are no vultures the Parsees cannot dispose of their dead, who were traditionally placed in special amphitheatres, where the vultures disposed of the corpses very quickly. In the absence of vultures, attempts have been made to direct the rays of the sun onto the corpses by using powerful mirrors. The Parsee religion forbids the pollution of the air by burning corpses, and the pollution of the earth by internment.

Why have so many vultures died? The culprit is 'Diclofenac', a drug widely used by vets and farmers for a variety of animal ailments. The drug, present in the bodies of dead animals, is consumed and attacks the bird's liver, and it then dies from a form of gout. The drug is now forbidden, a substitute drug is on the market, and numbers of vultures are on the increase.

A protected area of forest in Bangladesh, visited by the author in 2012, revealed 26 healthy birds and four active nests.

Eurasian Oystercatcher, *Haematopus ostralegus*, with prey.

Haematopus ostralegus
Eurasian Oystercatcher

The genus name is entirely from Ancient Greek. *Haimata* refers to the word for 'blood', and *pous* is the word for 'foot'.

The species name comes from *ostrea*, the Latin word for 'mussel' or 'oyster', and *legere*, the Latin verb 'to collect'.

Oystercatchers are known to practice 'egg-dumping'. Like the cuckoos, they sometimes deposit their eggs in gulls' nests and the young are then raised by the host species.

There are between 10 and 20 oystercatcher species around the world, depending on the taxonomy used, and each has an orange-red bill and either pied or all-blackish plumage.

Haliaeetus pelagicus
Steller's Sea Eagle

The genus name comes from New Latin, developed in Renaissance Italy following renewed interest in Greek and Roman civilisation. It is based on two Greek words: *hali* meaning 'sea', and *aetos* meaning 'eagle'.

The species name is based on the Latin word *pelagus*, meaning the 'ocean'.

Winter in Hokkaido, Japan, sees tourist boats braving high winds, temperatures down to -34°C (-30°F), and choppy seas to reach the ice-floes holding Steller's Sea Eagles. Chopped oily fish (chum) is scattered around the ice and the birds provide good photo opportunities as they devour their food.

It could be considered a mild form of 'extreme tourism', being just a bit more adventurous than a visit to the local nature reserve on a warm day, which ends with an ice cream on a park bench.

Black-breasted Buzzard, *Hamirostra melanosteron*, performing its party trick.

Hamirostra melanosteron
Black-breasted Buzzard

The genus name for this Australian species comes from the Latin word *hamatus*, which means 'furnished with a hook', and *rostrum*, the Latin word for a 'beak'.

The species name comes from *melanos*, the Greek word for 'black', and *sternum*, the Latin word for the 'breast-bone'. *Sterno* is a Latin word meaning 'to sneeze', making reference to the sternum, where the noise originates.

This bird of prey likes its eggs on the large side. Nests of birds such as bustards and emus are targeted for their eggs. The buzzard simply swoops on the host, and when the nesting bird flees terrified, the buzzard drops a stone or large object to break the eggs. The hapless parent can do nothing other than simply watch from a safe distance.

Hapaloptila castanea
White-faced Nunbird

Many birds are named after members of religious orders. There are cardinals in bright red, bishops in yellow or orange, nunbirds in black, monklets in sombre tones, capuchinbirds in brown, and tail-wagging hermits among the hummingbirds.

The White-faced Nunbird, a rare species of Andean forests, is the brightest of all those named after religious sisters. The genus name comes from *haphe*, a Latin word for 'fine sand', such as that used by wrestlers to dust their bodies. *Optila* comes from *optomai,* the future tense of the Greek verb 'to see'. Together they say that the plumage 'looks sandy'.

White-faced Nunbird, *Hapaloptila castanea*.

The awesome Harpy Eagle, *Harpia harpyja*.

The specific name also alludes to the colour of the plumage. *Castana* is the Spanish word for 'chestnut tree', and *castanea* is the name for a genus of chestnut trees.

Castanets, indeed, may have called the nuns to prayer during Lent, when bells were silent until Easter, and wooden boards were clapped together as a substitute.

Harpia harpyja
Harpy Eagle

The scientific name refers to the *harpies* in Greek mythology, and comes from the Greek verb *harpazo*, which means 'to steal'. The harpies were wind-spirits which took the souls of the deceased into eternity. They are depicted as winged women with ugly faces and the body and wings of a bird. They were thought to be responsible for sudden and mysterious disappearances, of people who had literally 'gone with the wind'.

In South America the Harpy Eagle is very well named. Monkeys and sloths are snatched (*harpazo*) from the trees, and held in powerful legs which are as thick as a human wrist. The wings are relatively short, to enable flight through the forest, and the long tail acts as a rudder for turning.

The bird is an 'apex predator', at the very top of the food chain, with talons much larger than the claws of a Jaguar or even a Grizzly Bear. Its presence in the forest is a good indicator of the health of the ecosystem. If the bird is thriving, then its prey is also doing well.

Sungrebe, *Heliornis fulica*.

Heliornis fulica
Sungrebe

The genus name comes from *helios*, the Greek word for the 'sun', and 'ornis', the Greek word for a 'bird'.

Fulica is a Latin word for the 'coot', from *fuligo*, meaning 'soot'. The Sungrebe is, literally, the brighter version of the coot.

This Latin American species has developed a unique protective mechanism for its young. The fledglings are born naked, blind and defenceless. The male has evolved skin pouches on the underside of the wing where they can clamber aboard for protection. The skin pouches are so compact that the youngsters can even be carried in flight.

Hippolais icterina
Icterine Warbler

The etymology of the species name is uncertain. *Hypo* can mean 'under' or 'over', and *lais* is the Greek word for a stone. Could it have anything to do with the Greek word *hippo*, which means 'horse'. Perhaps the carriage or shape of the head?

Icterus means 'yellow', and was an old name for jaundice. It was believed that the sight of the yellow bird mentioned by Aristotle, probably the Golden Oriole, would cure the disease.

Hirundapus caudacutus
White-throated Needletail

The genus name comes from the Latin word *hirundo,* which means 'swallow', and *apus,* the Greek word for 'swift'.

The species name comes from the Latin words *cauda*, which means 'tail', and *acuta*, which means 'sharp'.

An alternative English name for this species is Needle-tailed Swift. It has a large barrel-shaped body which can be hurled through the air at great speed. This species is considered the fastest bird of all in level flight, although others, such as the Peregrine Falcon, achieve greater speeds when they perform a stoop.

The White-throated Needletail breeds in Asia and southern Siberia, and winters south to Australia, although occasionally birds wander huge distances outside their usual range. For example, in June 2013 one arrived on the Hebridean island of

White-throated Needletail, *Hirundapus caudacutus* , taking a drink while on the wing.

Harris, in the UK. Birders visited from all over the country and around 40 of them watched in dismay as the bird flew into a wind-turbine and perished.

Hydrornis gurneyi
Gurney's Pitta

The genus name comes from two Greek words. *Hydro* comes from the word for 'water', as the birds breed in the wet season. *Ornis* is the word for 'bird'.

John Henry Gurney (1819–1890) after whom the bird was named, was at various times a banker, Liberal Member of Parliament, and writer who summarised the findings of travellers, but did very little fieldwork himself.

Pitta is the Greek word for 'cake'.

The Gurney's Pitta is one of the rarest and most sought-after species among birders who visit South-East Asia. A new population has been discovered in Burma, but sightings, despite stake-outs, are not always delivered. A community-based project aimed at raising awareness among local people has had little success and the population of these birds now appears to be dwindling. Illegal logging and deforestation and the widescale planting of palm oil plantations are to blame.

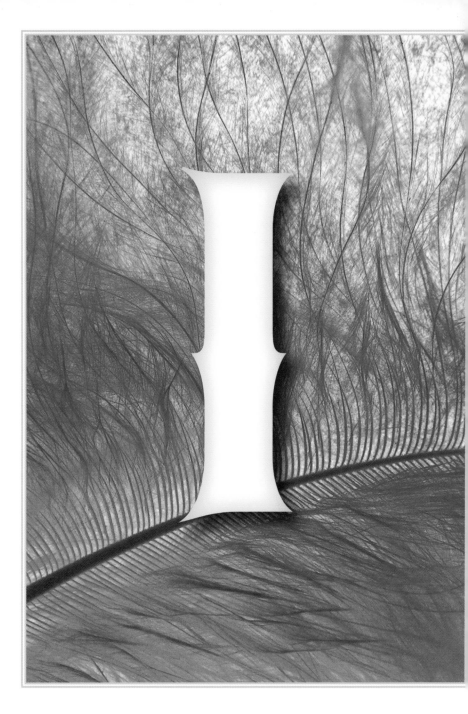

The beautiful black-and-gold male Baltimore Oriole, *Icterus galbula*.

Icterus galbula
Baltimore Oriole

Icteros is the Greek word for 'yellow'.

Galbula was a Latin word used to describe a yellow bird, presumed to be the Golden Oriole, which is an Old World species.

The word 'oriole' comes from the Latin word *aureolus*, meaning 'golden'.

The bird is the inspiration behind the Baltimore Orioles baseball team, and is also the state bird of Maryland.

Because of their beauty, many people attract these birds to their gardens with special oriole feeders. The birds are particularly fond of fresh fruit and grape jelly. It is the female who builds the hanging nest.

Ichthyaetus ichthyaetus
Great Black-headed Gull

The scientific name for this large and beautiful gull comes from two Greek words. *Ichthus* means 'fish', and *aetos* means 'eagle'.

Indicator indicator
Greater Honeyguide

The word *indicator* is the Latin for 'pointer'. The honeyguide, as its name suggests, has a single favourite food, honey.

A Taste of Honey

The honeyguide's claws are too weak to tear open the nests of bees, but help is at hand. A series of notes will alert a human passer-by, who will then follow the bird to the golden treasure. The hive may be smoked in order to avoid bee stings. The human assistant then opens the hive, usually with a panga or sharp blade, and helps himself to the contents. The honeyguide will feast on the leftovers.

Members of the Boran tribe in Kenya call the honeyguide with a sharp whistle. When the bird appears and responds with a call, the hunting expedition sets off. On arrival the bird gives quite a different call, an 'indication' that the nest is near.

For all its 'sweet tooth', the Greater Honeyguide has a barbarous side. It is a 'brood-parasite' and a female will lay as many as 20 eggs every year, always in the nests of other birds. When the chick hatches, the powerful hook at the end of its bill is used to inflict wounds to kill the other nestlings.

The Ratel, or Honey Badger, will often eat alongside the honeyguide, but as yet evidence is scant that the badger is led there by the bird.

The 'reed-bellower', better known as *Ixobrychus minutus* or the Little Bittern.

Irania gutturalis
White-throated Robin

The genus name refers to the country Iran, where the bird is common, and *gutturalis,* a Latin word, meaning 'of the throat'.

Ixobrychus minutus
Little Bittern

The genus name comes from *ixias*, the Greek word for a 'reed', and

bruchomein, the Greek verb 'to bellow'.

The specific name is the Latin word for 'small'.

This is a tiny heron which can easily perch on a reed, although the alleged 'bellow' sound is rather misleading since the 'song' is more of a croak. Perhaps there was some confusion with its larger cousin, the Great Bittern, which makes a booming sound like a foghorn.

The cryptic plumage of the Eurasian Wryneck, *Jynx torquilla,* offers perfect camouflage against a trunk or log.

Jynx torquilla
Eurasian Wryneck

*Iunx i*s the Greek name for the 'wryneck'.

Tortus is the Latin word for 'twisting', and *collis* is the Latin name for an 'elevation'.

When holding migrant Wryneck in the hand, for ringing purposes, ornithologists are astonished as the neck is twisted around 180°, and moves laterally and horizontally during the activity. This snake-like movement is used to deter intruders at the nest, and causes no injury to the bird. The same cannot be said for humans, as the condition 'wryneck', or 'torticollis', is a feared medical diagnosis which is very painful and requires therapy.

A Great Grey Shrike, *Lanius excubitor*, impaling its prey.

Lanius collurio
Red-backed Shrike

Lanius is the Latin for 'butcher'.

Collurio is the Greek word for a bird mentioned by Aristotle.

The English name shrike comes from the word 'shriek', making reference to the bird's call.

The Red-backed shrike is a predator of small birds, frogs, lizards and rodents. Like other shrikes it hunts from prominent perches and impales prey on thorns or barbed wire. In other words, what isn't eaten is stored in a 'larder' for future use.

– L. excubitor
Great Grey Shrike

Excubitor is the Latin word for 'watchman'.

Like other members of the genus, this shrike uses exposed perches for hunting and will store food. If the bird recognises that its prey contains toxic chemicals, it will be left impaled for several days until the chemicals are degraded. Great Grey Shrikes are well aware that the skin of a toad is poisonous, and have been seen pulling the skin over the creature's head and discarding it to avoid contamination.

– *L. nubicus*
Masked Shrike

Nubicus is a geographical term and makes reference to the Nubian region bordering the Nile.

The Masked Shrike's breeding range extends from south-east Europe to the Middle East, and the species winters in north-east Africa. It is the smallest of all the shrikes, hunting from less exposed perches, and impaling prey on a 'larder of thorns'.

Larus argentatus
European Herring Gull

The genus name is the Latin for a gull or other seabird.

The species name *argentatus* is a Latin word meaning 'silvery'.

This gull has adapted to live in towns, nesting on the roofs of buildings and frequenting refuse dumps, and sometimes snatching food from unsuspecting holidaymakers. They have also learned to dance on grassy areas, mimicking the patter of raindrops, so that worms are lured to the surface in order to help feed an enormous appetite.

After hatching, the red spot on the parent's bill is an invitation for the chicks to feed. They peck at the spot instinctively until the adults regurgitate food.

Leiopa ocellata
Malleefowl

The Malleefowl is a member of the megapode family, a name literally meaning 'big-feet'. *Pes* is the Latin word for 'foot', and *mega* comes from *meganistes*, the Latin word for 'grandees' or 'important people'.

Mallee is the name of a group of eucalyptus trees that grow in Australia.

The species name comes from the Latin word *oculus* meaning 'eye', and refers to the eye-like markings on the bird's plumage.

While the modern poultry farmer uses an artificial incubator, nature developed one for the Malleefowl long before humans arrived on the scene.

The parent Malleefowl build mounds of leaves and moss around 1.5m (5ft) high, and 3m (10ft) across. Eggs are buried inside these 'furnaces', where the heat can rise to 38°C (100°F). The male will constantly check the temperature by probing his beak deep inside like a thermometer. As soon as the heat inside reaches the limit, the male will open the mound with his huge feet, to cool off the inside.

When the young hatch, the parents are nowhere to be seen. Unaided, they claw their way to the surface and can immediately begin to feed. It may take up to 15 hours for a young bird to escape the nest, but after that the chick is able to run well within an hour, can flutter a short distance within two hours, and fly quite well within a day.

Leucogeranus leucogeranus
Siberian Crane

The genus and specific names come from the Greek word *leuco*, meaning 'white', and the Latin verb *gerere*, 'to bear'.

Leucophaeus atricilla
Laughing Gull

The genus name comes from two Greek words. *Leuco* means 'white', and *phaeus* means 'dusky'.

The species name comes from two Latin words. *Ater* means 'black', and the suffix *cilla* gives it a diminutive form.

This is an American gull, with a fuller and darker hood than the European Black-headed Gull. Like most gulls it has a keen appetite and will eat almost anything, including garbage in an advanced state of decay and offal from fishing vessels. They nest in groups on islands near the shore, to avoid the theft of eggs and chicks by rats and other terrestrial predators.

The call is reminiscent of a high-pitched laugh from a sore throat. For a number of years an individual resided in the UK (where it is a very rare bird) on grass outside Newcastle General Hospital. Was it looking for the ear, nose and throat department?

Leucopsar rothschildi
Bali Myna

The genus name comes from the Greek word for 'white eye-browed'.

The specific name pays tribute to the British ornithologist Walter Rothschild (1868–1937).

The Bali Myna pays a great price for its loveliness. Such is the lust for rare birds as captive trophies that less than 100 survive in the wild. This is despite supreme efforts on the part of the government to increase the population. Selected breeders are given a package of 15 males and 15 females to breed in captivity. By agreement, 10 per cent of the fledglings are returned to the wild, while the remainder can legally become part of the cagebird trade. The problem is that hundreds of released birds fall captive to poachers. Around 1,000 birds are caged legally, but huge numbers are kept illegally as household pets.

The Critically Endangered Bali Myna,
Leucopsar rothschildi.

The Bar-tailed Godwit, *Limosa lapponica*, is the ultimate long-distance migrant.

A World Traveller

The Bar-tailed Godwit is rather plain in appearance, but as an athlete its statistics are spectacular. One bird was tracked from New Zealand to the Yellow Sea in China, and covered a distance of 11,051km (6,851 miles) in nine days at an average of 1,228km (760 miles) per day.

Prior to migration the godwit will feast voraciously on crustaceans and sandworms. When the conditions are deemed right, with a following wind, the bird sets off and loses half its body weight on the journey. An ability to fly virtually non-stop is helped by the godwit's ability to sleep on the wing, with one side of the brain shut down. Because they do not eat on migration, the organs used for digestion are dormant and become absorbed into the body. Some of the alimentary canal, with the kidneys and liver, are then reconstituted into their proper places at the end of the journey.

The act of 'eating its own body' has a scientific name. 'Autophagy' comes from two Greek words. *Autos* is the 'self'. *Phagein* is the verb 'to eat'.

Limosa lapponica
Bar-tailed Godwit
Limus is the Latin word for 'mud', and *lapponica* is a geographical term meaning 'Lapland'.

Linaria cannabina
Common Linnet

Linaria is the Latin name for a weaver of flax.

Cannabina resonates with the word cannabis, and has the same Latin root: *Cannabina* means 'hemp' (another street name for cannabis). The bird is partial to seeds from the flax plant. Does the word 'addicted' fit here?

– L. flavirostris
Twite

A close relative of the linnet, with a distinctive pinkish rump, which tends to breed in open habitats and favours higher ground. The species name *flavirostris* makes reference to the yellowish colour of the bill. *Rostrum* means 'beak' in Latin and *flavea* means 'yellowish'.

Acanthis flavirostris, the Twite, showing its strawberry-coloured rump.

Locustella lanceolata
Lanceoloted Warbler

Locusta is the Latin word for a 'grasshopper'. *Ella* gives the word a diminutive form.

The specific name comes from *lancea*, the Latin word for a 'spear', and makes reference to the streaks on its breast.

The 'lancey', as the bird is affectionately known, is hard to see unless it begins to sing. The song is a monotonous insect-like reeling, as in other *Locustella* warblers. Although it is often called a 'Sibe', short for Siberian, the Lanceoloted Warbler has a wide breeding range that extends from Finland through Asia to Kamchatka and Japan, and winters south to Bangladesh and South-East Asia.

Most British records come from Shetland, especially Fair Isle, where it is a skulking vagrant hiding in long grass. Nothing quite stirs the blood as the word 'lancey', uttered in some wet field on Fair Isle in the month of September.

The crossed mandibles of the Red Crossbill, *Loxia curvirostra*.

But once located the bird is tame, and has even crawled over the muddy boots of twitchers as they add it to their lists.

Loxia curvirostra
Red Crossbill

The genus name comes from *loxos*, a Greek word for 'crosswise'.

The species name comes from the Latin verb *curvus,* meaning 'to bend', and *rostrum*, meaning 'beak'.

The upper mandible can bend either to the left or the right. There is much variation in bill size and call note,

The Scottish Crossbill, *Loxia curvirostra scotica*.

leading to some claims that there are as many as nine separate crossbill species in the Americas alone. In simple terms, a 'lumper' would score a single Red Crossbill on their list, a 'splitter' would divide the bird into several species, giving their lifelist a higher score. For example, the Scottish Crossbill (*L.c. scotica*) was formerly considered a separate species by some authorities due to variations in bill size and vocalisation.

As early as 1857, Charles Darwin put it succinctly. In a letter to a friend, he wrote that 'those who make many species are the splitters, and those who make few are the lumpers'. DNA testing has put the matter on a more scientific basis.

– *L. pytyopsittacus*
Parrot Crossbill

The species name comes from two Greek words. *Pitus* means 'pine', and *psittakos* means 'parrot'.

This species has a bill which is noticeably larger and deeper than that of the Red Crossbill, together with a bigger body and a distinctive deeper call-note.

Luscinia calliope
Siberian Rubythroat

The genus name is the Latin word for a 'nightingale'.

The species name comes from *Calliope*, a Muse in Greek mythology who presided over eloquence and poetry.

The Siberian Rubythroat breeds in Siberia, and then migrates to India,

A Jack Snipe, *Lymnocryptes minimus,* stands in front of its larger relative.

Thailand and Indonesia, where the insect population is abundant in winter.

More and more Siberian birds which were once classified as rare now appear in good numbers further west. This lovely bird had almost achieved mythical status in the UK, but in the past couple of decades it has begun to put in regular appearances, even though it remains a great rarity.

– *L. megarhynchos*
Common Nightingale

Megarhynchus comes from Ancient Greek. *Mega* is the Greek word for 'large', and *rhynchus* is the word for 'beak'.

The Common Nightingale is a migrant to Western Europe, including southern Britain. Males arrive before the females and set up their territory. The females arrive later, as night migrants, and are attracted to the males which sing throughout the night. The song, which ends in a crescendo, is one of the loveliest sounds in nature, inspiring poets and playwrights.

Lymnocryptes minimus
Jack Snipe

The genus name comes from *limne*, the Greek word for a 'marsh', and *kruptos*, the Greek word for 'hidden'. It is a fitting name as the Jack Snipe hides well in wetland vegetation and will remain out of sight unless disturbed.

The species name is the Latin word for 'smallest', and the Jack Snipe is sometimes known as the 'half-snipe'. Jack is a common word to describe anything diminutive.

The Jack Snipe inhabits the genus *Lymnocryptus* all by itself, as the sternum is quite different from the breastbone of other snipe species. If flushed it flies low, in a flight unlike the towering zigzag flight of a flushed Common Snipe, and settles back in the marsh after a short distance.

Common Nightingale, *Luscinia megarhynchos* – brown plumage but a big mouth, and a big voice to match!

Female Bee Hummingbird, *Mellisuga helenae.*

Manacus vitellinus
Golden-collared Manakin

The genus name comes from the Dutch word *Mannikin*, meaning 'little man'. The specific name comes from the Latin word *vitellus*, meaning a little calf, referring to the large head. They are found in Panama and western Colombia.

Golden-collared Manakins have an astonishing courtship dance. A number of males gather around leaf litter and dance. The word 'moonwalk', as popularised by Michael Jackson, would perfectly describe their movements, as they glide backwards over the branches. At the same time, these 'jungle-dancers' snap their wings together over their backs, to produce clicking, humming and snapping sounds. Every stop is pulled out, to blow the female's mind.

Mellisuga helenae
Bee Hummingbird

The genus name comes from two Latin words. *Mel* means 'honey', and *sugere* is the verb 'to suck in'.

The species is reputedly named after Helen Booth, a friend of Juan Gundlach (1810–1896), who was an eminent ornithologist in Cuba.

The Bee Hummingbird is the smallest bird in the world. The male is slightly shorter than the female, being a mere 5cm (2in) in length. It would take 18 males to tip the scales at 30g (1oz). Close inspection of this Cuban speciality will reveal a 'living jewel', with fiery red throat and iridescent gorget.

Yet despite its tiny size, the Bee Hummingbird is a strong and swift flier, and has been clocked at 50kph (30mph).

A flock of wild 'budgies'.

It feeds by probing its bill deep into nectar-producing flowers, carrying pollen from one bush to the next and helping plants to propagate. The bird is too small to maintain its body temperature at night, so the tiny hummingbird enters into a state of torpor to reduce its energy needs.

Melopsittacus undulata
Budgerigar

The genus name comes from Greek and means 'melodious parrot'.

The specific name comes from the Latin word for 'wavy'.

The 'budgie', to give it its household name, is popular as a cagebird and is endlessly entertaining, with as much personality, ounce for ounce, as any living creature. Birds can whistle and interact with humans, and are the third most popular pet in the world after the cat and the dog. Males in particular have a gift of mimicry, and can amass a vocabulary of dozens of words.

In the wild, when flocks are harried by a bird of prey, they bunch together in a tight formation. The predator then finds it hard to target an individual bird.

Menura novaehollandiae
Superb Lyrebird

The genus name comes from the Greek word *miniskos*, which means 'crescent' and refers to the markings on the male's tail feathers.

The species name is geographical as 'New Holland' was an original name for Australia.

The English name comes from the spectacular tail feathers, which are spread over the back as the male sings.

Mergus serrator
Red-breasted
Merganser

The genus *Mergus* comes from an unspecified bird mentioned by Pliny.

Serra is the Latin word for 'saw'. These fish-eating ducks have serrated edges to their bills, to prevent slippery fish from escaping, and are commonly known as 'sawbills'. Mergansers have been seen hunting collectively, encircling fish and driving them into shallow water, where they are easily caught.

The English name comes from *mergus* and *anser*, with the latter meaning 'goose'.

Merops apiaster
European Bee-eater

The genus name comes from *mel*, the Latin word for honey, and *ops*, from the Greek verb 'to look at'.

It's little wonder that the European Bee-eater, *Merops apiaster*, is also known as the 'rainbow bird'.

The species name comes from *apis,* the Latin word for a 'bee'. Aristotle advised beekeepers to kill the bird, if they wanted their apiaries to thrive.

The bee-eater is a lovely and unmistakeable bird. In some cultures they are associated with gossip and scandalmongering, as if their conversations with each other have a 'sting' in the mouth. So enjoy these exotic birds, even close up, but be careful what you say!

– M. persicus
Blue cheeked Bee-eater

The species name is geographical, and means Persian. The staple diet of the Blue-cheeked Bee-eater is dragonflies, which it often hunts from an open perch.

Mimicry: To Capture Her Heart

It is remarkable that Australia produces such an array of singing birds. The Superb Lyrebird has no equal in the mimicry stakes. In the course of a few minutes, a single bird in the wild can mimic the kookaburra so convincingly that the real bird responds. Add to that the songs of 20 other birds, and you have a memory like a computer. Into that mix you can throw the sound of a chainsaw, a mobile phone, the shutter on a camera, a car siren, and many more. It seems that females are attracted to the most varied voices, and the brightest plumes. If the male can do a convincing dance on the forest floor, he has captured her heart.

Micromonacha lanceolata
Lanceolated Monklet

The genus name comes from *micros*, a Greek adjective for 'small', and *monazein*, a Greek verb meaning 'to live alone'. Various forms of the Greek verb appear in the scientific names of birds, referring to the solitary, enclosed status of some religious brothers and sisters.

The specific name comes from *lancea*, the Latin word for a 'spear', and refers to the streaked markings on the body.

The author remembers long and fruitless hours looking for the monklet in Costa Rica. The scientific name suits well as the bird is mainly quiet, as if it has taken a vow of silence, and spends long hours sitting patiently, as if in prayer, in the canopy.

Lanceolated Monklet, *Micromonacha lanceolata*.

Similarly, the English name refers to the bird's appearance as a small (and well-fed!) monk.

Milvus milvus
Red Kite

The genus name is the Latin word for the kite, and probably comes from *miles*, the word for a soldier, and refers to its 'plunder' of anything edible. *Milvinus* is a Latin word meaning 'rapacious'.

Mimus polyglottos
Northern Mockingbird

The genus name is the Latin word for a 'farce', or a 'mime actor'.

The specific name is based on two Greek words: *poly* means 'many', and *glossa* means 'language'.

The bird, literally, is a 'polyglot' which can speak a number of languages, and can mimic the calls and songs of other birds, but also noises as bizarre as squeaking wheels, frogs and musical instruments. To have a mockingbird flaunting his vocals in the garden is like having birds of several different species outside the window, accompanied sometimes on the piano.

Monasa morphoeus
White-fronted Nunlet

The genus name comes from the Greek verb *monazein*, which means 'to live alone', or *mona*, an adjective pertaining to a single woman.

The specific name comes from *morphe*, the Greek noun for 'shape'.

The Northern Mockingbird, *Mimus polyglottos*, has subdued plumage but a remarkable voice.

With black gown and white wimple, a 'nunnish' impression may be given, but this bird is noisy and gregarious. A flock of several birds will set up a rollicking chorus, with heads thrown back for dramatic effect, of various gobbling and barking notes (more like Whoopee Goldberg in *Sister Act*!). The birds travel with other species, along with a flock sentinel to sound the alarm if danger approaches. In Costa Rica the author noticed that they fly with flocks of other birds such as caciques and oropendolas. Waves of feeding birds are often preceded by tanager species at the front, and sometimes troupes of travelling monkeys which flush prey for the birds to eat. Small frogs and lizards which escape the monkeys will fall into the clutches of feeding birds.

Monticola saxatilis
Common Rock-thrush

The genus name comes from two Latin words. *Mons* is the word for 'mountain', and *colere* is the verb 'to dwell'. *Monticola* is the Latin for a mountaineer.

The species name also comes from two Latin words. *Saxum* means 'rock', and *collis* means 'elevation'.

Montifringilla davidiana
Père David's Snowfinch

The genus name comes from two Latin words: *mons* is the word for 'mountain', *fringilla* is the word for a 'finch'.

The species is named after Père David (1826–1900), the French priest and scientist who listed 63 new species of flora and fauna in Mongolia, China and Tibet. We also have Père David's Deer and Père David's Rat-Snake.

Père David had been trained in zoology and botany. When he was sent to China by his superiors in 1860, he was invited by the scientific community to bring back specimens for the Natural History Museum in Paris. He collected over 900 skins of birds, and was the first to describe no less than 65 species. He is also credited as the first European to cast eyes on the Giant Panda.

Morus bassanus
Northern Gannet

The genus name comes from an ancient Greek word meaning 'foolish', due to the ease with which nesting birds allow themselves to be caught and killed.

The species is named after the Bass Rock, an island in the Firth of Forth, Scotland, where more than 70,000 pairs of gannets breed.

The English name comes from an Old English word, *ganot*, which means 'strong' or 'manly'.

The gannet plunges for fish from as high as 30m (100ft), and pursues the prey underwater. To cushion the blow there are air sacs on the face and chest which act like 'bubble-wrapping'. The eyes are positioned well forward in the face, binocular-style, allowing the bird to judge distances better.

Young gannets, called 'guga', are eaten on Lewis, a Hebridean Island, and by law 2,000 can be taken annually. The 'guga' hunts go back to the Iron Age. Despite this practice, the number of gannets breeding on the island has doubled over the past 30 years.

Motacilla cinerea
Grey Wagtail

The genus name comes from the Latin verb *motare*, 'to move about'. The final two syllables have a diminutive meaning.

Cinerea comes from *cineres*, the Latin word for 'ashes', but the bird is much prettier than its name suggests. The combination of slate-grey and lemon-yellow composes a lovely picture.

The Grey Wagtail is constantly in motion, and often seen beside flowing water. The flight is undulating, and the tail is longer than that of most other species in the wagtail family. The tail is never at rest, constantly wagging as the stern moves along with it.

In summer Bass Rock is turned white with the bodies of tens of thousands of nesting gannets.

Egyptian Vulture, *Neophron percnopterus*, soaring on blue-black wings.

Neophron percnopterus
Egyptian Vulture

The genus name comes from Greek mythology. In a story of love and deception, the evil *Neophron* is turned by the gods into a vulture as punishment.

The specific name comes from *perknos*, the Greek word for 'blue-black', and *pterux*, the Greek word for a 'wing'.

In Spain the habit of 'coprophagy' (eating excrement) has given the Egyptian Vulture the name *churretero*, the 'dung-eater'. In Egyptian hieroglyphics the bird represented royalty, and as a protected bird in pharaonic times it inherited the name 'pharaoh's chicken'.

Nestor notabilis
Kea

The species name is a Latin word for 'noteworthy', and the English name is the Maori word for this mountain parrot, based on its loud screech.

The species name is apposite, as the bird is 'noteworthy' for several reasons. The Kea is highly intelligent and can prepare and use tools to obtain food. It is also the world's only alpine parrot, and its notorious urge to explore and manipulate makes it a menace on the ski-slopes, tearing open rucksacks and picnic hampers. In addition it has a liking for pulling off the rubber seals around the windows of cars parked on the New Zealand slopes.

The Kea, *Nestor notabilis*, demonstrates one of its noteworthy habits.

Clark's Nutcracker, *Nucifraga columbiana*.

Nucifraga caryocatactes
Spotted Nutcracker

The genus word comes from *nucleus*, meaning 'kernel', and *frangere*, meaning 'to shatter'. The species name simply repeats that information, this time in Greek. *Karyon* is the word for 'nut', and *kateseio* is the word for 'to shatter'.

The nutcracker has a bill which is specialised for extracting seeds from pine cones. Surplus food is stored, and the birds seem to remember where it is hidden, even when covered in snow. These are the seeds which will reforest an area after a forest fire, or degradation by human activity.

– *N. columbiana*
Clark's Nutcracker

The species name is geographical, being an old name for 'America'.

This is a high mountain bird, found among pine forests in 'Columbia' and elsewhere in the west. In flight the wings are broad and floppy, as the bird searches for pine cones. The long dagger–shaped bill rips open the cones, and seeds are stored in a pouch under the tongue. Tens of thousands of seeds are stored around the forest, the large number being an insurance policy against thieving squirrels. The bird has a wonderful memory and knows months later where the food is stashed. This bird, as we might say, is a hard nut to crack.

Numenius tenuirostris
Slender-billed Curlew

The genus name comes from the Latin word *numen*, meaning a 'divinity'.

The species name comes from two Latin words: *tenuis* means 'thin', and *rostrum* means 'bill'.

The Slender-billed Curlew is unique in that it has been added to the 'British List' twice (see 'The Hastings Rarities' box below), and deleted twice.

With no verified sighting for more than two decades there is a strong possibility that this species is now extinct.

The Hastings Rarities

A taxidermist in Hastings, George Bristow (1863–1947), claimed to have been given the skins of more than 500 rare birds of 30 species shot locally between 1892–1930, and among them was a single Slender-billed Curlew. In reality these specimens were shot abroad and smuggled into the country, and selling them made Bristow a rich man to the tune of £7,000. The fraud was discovered in the 1960s.

Most of the birds that were new to Britain and subsequently struck off have

The 'nocturnal raven' – better known as the Black-crowned Night Heron, *Nycticorax nycticorax*.

Nycticorax nycticorax
Black-crowned Night Heron

The scientific name comes from *nox* the Latin noun for 'night'. *Noctis* is the genitive case of the noun, and means 'of the night', or 'nocturnal'. The second part of the name comes from *corax*, the Greek word for a 'raven'.

Nymphicus hollandicus
Cockatiel

The genus name *nymphicus* refers to the 'nymphs' in Greek mythology. Visitors to Australia felt this name did justice to the charisma of the bird.

The specific name refers to New Holland, the old name for Australia.

The Cockatiel is the most popular household bird after the Budgerigar. The crest tells of the bird's mood. When the crest is raised, the bird is excited, when semi-flattened, it is relaxed, and when flattened, angry.

been reinstated with, for example, Cory's Shearwater sometimes seen in good numbers, and Cetti's Warbler firmly established as a British resident. And the Slender-billed Curlew? It's a case of 'on, off, on, off – considered unproven'.

A bird which appeared in Druridge Bay, Northumberland, in 1998, was considered by many to be a Slender-billed Curlew – perhaps the last one seen anywhere in the world. Although it was seen well, photographed and videoed, the sighting, which was originally accepted, was eventually rejected on the grounds of insufficient evidence.

Oenanthe oenanthe
Northern Wheatear

The scientific name comes from two Greek words. *Oinos* is the word for 'wine', and *anthos* is the word for 'flower'. The name celebrates the Northern Wheatear's return to Greece in the springtime, just as the grapevines begin to blossom.

The English name is a corruption of the two words, 'white' and 'arse', and was used from the 16th century.

The wheatear feeds on the ground, frequently bobbing its tail and hawking for flies. The rump is conspicuously white.

A 19th century artwork of a pair of Northern Wheatears, *Oenanthe oenanthe*.

– O. deserti
Desert Wheatear

The genus name refers to its favoured habitat, the desert. A small bush or tuft of grass provides the perfect perch from which to spot a beetle or caterpillar for consumption.

This is the only wheatear which has a white rump, and no white extending down the tail, and so is easy to identify. It is a rare vagrant to Western Europe, but is now seen annually in Britain.

Opisthocomus hoazin
Hoatzin

The genus name comes from Greek, meaning 'wearing long hair behind'.

The prehistoric-looking Hoatzin, *Opisthocomus hoazin*.

The specific name comes from *uatzin*, an Aztec word for a pheasant or gamebird.

The Hoatzin is also known as the 'stink bird'. This unlovely name refers to the foul smell caused by the fermentation of food in its digestive system. The diet is almost exclusively leaves, but these are hard to digest and the process takes time in a huge foregut which serves this sole purpose. As the foregut is heavy long flights are impossible, but thankfully there is an abundance of leaves in Amazonia so there is no need to forage far for food.

The 'song' is impossible to transcribe on a standard clef. A series of grunts, followed by hisses, groans and croaks, is the closest to a description of its music.

It is difficult to pinpoint exactly where the Hoatzin fits into the bird kingdom. In appearance it seems to have a bit of pigeon, a sprinkle of cuckoo, perhaps a feather or two of rail. In fact the bird has a niche all to itself and *Opisthocomus* is a genus the Hoatzin shares with no other species. And for all its oddity, it does have a certain homeliness. After all it has been chosen, above gorgeous hummingbirds and tanagers, as the national bird of Guyana.

Oriolus oriolus
Golden Oriole

The scientific name comes from the Latin word *aureolus* which means 'golden'. The striking yellow and black plumage of the male is replaced by a drabber green in the female. The song is transcribed as a lovely fluting 'wee-wee-oo'.

The summer diet is mainly caterpillars. The larva is shaken up and down, and from side to side, to remove the hairs, and then the food is eaten. In winter the diet is mainly fruit and berries, although the bird has been seen stealing from the larders of shrikes.

A Wild Owl Chase

Finding the Anjouan Scops-Owl requires sure footing, a good torch, an ability to mimic, and a chunk of luck. The author recalls a rather scary climb at dusk in June 2016, then sitting under a stake-out for three hours before the tiny owl, at 18cm (7in) long, was lured by a plaintive whistle and settled above our heads. Very soon it was off to continue its murderous attacks on local rodents and insects. The head shape, seen clearly in torchlight, was large and did indeed seem like a *nodus* ('knot') on the head.

Slithering back down the slope in the wake of a very sure-footed guide could only lead to one destination, equivalent to the 19th hole on a golf course: a local restaurant with a cold beer, to celebrate a bird that had 'come back from the dead'.

Otis tarda
Great Bustard

The genus word comes from *otium*, the Latin word for leisure, and *tarda*, the Latin word for slow. The male sports a fine moustache, and its great bulk prevents fast movements. Nor is it in any hurry to reach full maturity. This can take five years.

Otus capnodes
Anjouan Scops-Owl

Otus is the Latin for 'eared owl'.

The species name comes from two Latin words: *caput* is the word for 'head', and *nodus* means 'knot'.

Since Madagascar, along with other islands including the Comoros, Mauritius, Seychelles and Réunion, broke off from East Africa some 60 million years ago, a different species of scops-owl has evolved on practically every island, no matter how small.

In the Comoros, the Anjouan Scops-Owl went missing for around 100 years, but was rediscovered in 1992.

Oxyura jamaicensis
Ruddy Duck

The genus name comes from two Greek words. *Oxus* means 'sharp', and *oura* means 'tail'. These are 'stiff-tailed' ducks from the Americas.

The species name is geographical.

The drake Ruddy Duck,
Oxyura jamaicensis,
is a striking bird.

Ruddy Duck versus White-headed Duck

Escapees from wildfowl collections led to an explosion of Ruddy Duck numbers in the UK, which then spread to Europe, where the birds interbred with the endangered White-headed Duck. A scheme to extirpate them has seen UK numbers reduced from several thousand to less than 100 in 2016.

The scheme has been hugely controversial, and opponents say that it is based on several false notions. Whatever the case, these are lovely birds, which were originally brought into the country because of their colourful plumage.

Osprey, *Pandion haliaetus*, with a catch.

Pagophila eburnea
Ivory Gull

The genus name comes from *pagos*, the Greek word for 'sea-ice', and *phileo*, the Greek verb 'to love'.

The species name is the Latin word for 'ivory-coloured'.

Today this lovely bird with snowy-white plumage is in decline. Perhaps the disappearance of sea-ice is the cause, although the Ivory Gull has long been hunted for food. Arctic explorers reported that its flesh was delicious. During S.A. Andrée's (1854–1897) ill-fated attempt to reach the North Pole by balloon in 1897, the diaries of the deceased contained accounts of Ivory Gulls being shot and eaten.

Pandion haliaetus
Osprey

Pandion was the legendary Greek king of Athens. Why the biologist Savigny (1779–1861), writing in 1809, chose to name the Osprey after a Greek king remains a mystery. Although the mythical king had three daughters, all of whom met tragic ends. Procne was transformed into a swallow, and Philomela into a nightingale. The king's punishment for his lifelong cruelty was to spend eternity searching for his two daughters. There is a regal quality to the Osprey, as it quarters high above the water, hunting endlessly.

The species name comes from the Greek word *hali*, which means 'sea', and *aetos*, which means 'eagle'.

The eye-catching Blue Bird-of-Paradise, *Paradisaea rudolphi*.

Paradisaea rudolphi
Blue Bird-of-Paradise

The *genus* name comes from *paradeisos*, the Greek word for 'garden'.

The species is named after the Crown Prince Rudolf of Austria (1858–1889).

There are many birds considered as the most beautiful in the world, and the Blue Bird-of-Paradise is on many peoples' shortlists, being one of the most eyecatching members of a stunning family.

When the sailors of Magellan's 16th century expedition returned with skins there was great excitement at the Spanish court. The forest seemed an unworthy place for such glory, so the sailors called them birds-of-paradise. The skins had no feet, as local hunters had simply cut them off, seeing no need for them. The Spaniards thought, therefore, that they could not have walked upon the earth, and must have originated somewhere heavenly.

The Blue Bird-of-Paradise is endemic to Papua New Guinea, where chieftains used its feathers to indicate their rank, and latterly they were exported to India to adorn the heads of the maharajas. Before long they arrived in Europe, where dandified young men paid large sums of gold for a few feathers.

Parus major
Great Tit

The genus name is the Latin word for 'tit'. The specific name is the Latin word for 'greater'.

The Great Tit has been much studied. The wide vocal repertoire has led to the 'Beau Geste' theory. In the book of the same name by P.C. Wren, the hero places dead soldiers upright against the walls of the desert fort, to give the impression it is well protected. The multiple calls of the Great Tit perhaps suggest he has a 'presence' equal to that of several birds.

It seems that females prefer to choose a male with a wide black apron, and brighter coloured birds do better in the mating game. The brightness of yellow on the breast depends upon carotenoids, a colour variable achieved by food-choice.

Great Tits are intelligent birds, and have been seen using pine needles as tools to prise larvae from tree holes. When feeding young, adult Great Tits will remove the gut from caterpillars, as the gut contains tannin, which is toxic to the young birds.

Passer domesticus
House Sparrow

The genus name is the Latin word for a sparrow.

The specific name comes from *domus*, the Latin word for a 'dwelling'.

Few birds are more closely associated with people than the House Sparrow. This is a noisy, gregarious bird whose success comes from its ability to eat a varied diet

House Sparrows, *Passer domesticus*, share our homes around the world.

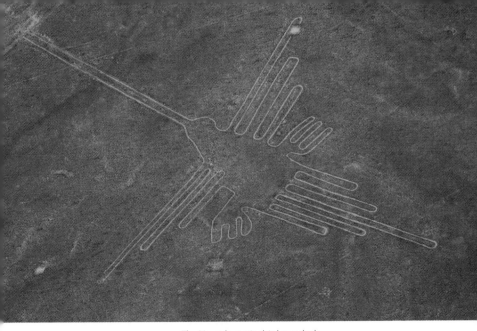

The Nazca hummingbird geoglyph.

and nest anywhere. It has spread to every continent except Antarctica. They collect our leftovers at outdoor cafes and picnic spots, and are among the world's most opportunistic birds.

Patagona gigas
Giant Hummingbird

Patagona is a geographical name, and *gigas* is the Latin word for giant.

This is a high-altitude bird of the Andes that is plentiful at high-altitude tourist spots such as Lake Titicaca on the Peru-Bolivia border.

To conserve energy these birds are capable of entering a state of torpor, often for hours on end. During cold spells, or if the food supply is poor, this is a necessary survival tool. After egg-laying, to replace the calcium lost, the females will augment their diet, adding salt, soil and slaked lime. Nectar is low in vitamins, and flies and other insects are eaten to make up the shortfall.

The Giant Hummingbird has a cultural significance for the Mapuche people, who believe that a woman who captures the bird will become fertile.

The Nazca hummingbird geoglyph appears to use *P. gigas* as a template. The hummingbird is one of a series of art works scratched into the ground, with others depicting birds, flowers, animals, and so on. Their purpose is unclear, but according to current theory they were used as water rituals in a desert where water has never been abundant.

Pelecanus crispus
Dalmatian Pelican

The genus name comes from *pelacos,* the Greek word for an 'axe', and is descriptive of the bird's bill-shape.

The species name, the Latin word *crispus*, means 'curly-haired' after the bird's crest.

'What a wonderful bird is the pelican, its beak holds more than its belly can'. The children's ditty is a trifle misleading, as the famous elastic pouch catches fish, and then the bill is tipped backwards, up to 14 litres (3 gallons) of water are flushed out, and the fish is consumed.

These are among the heaviest birds in the world, but are graceful in flight.

Pelicans feed exclusively on fish, and are sometimes shot by fishermen who believe that they deplete fish stocks. In Mongolia Dalmatian Pelicans are killed and their bills sold as pouches. On any market day in Mongolia buyers will find as many as 40 pelican bills for sale. The number of Dalmatian Pelicans in Mongolia is now down to just 130, while the world population stands at about 30,000 birds.

Close-up of the crazy crest of the Dalmatian Pelican, *Pelecanus crispus.*

Perdix perdix
Grey Partridge

The scientific name comes from a story in Homer's *The Odyssey*. Perdix was the nephew of Daedalus, a master craftsman. Under his tuition, Perdix was so successful in his wondrous creations that his uncle, in a fit of jealousy, threw him over the side of the Acropolis. As he plummeted to earth, the Goddess Athene turned him into a partridge. Today the whirring wings of the Grey Partridge give the bird many a reprieve as it flies to escape the hawk's talons or the hunter's shots.

Perissocephalus tricolor
Capuchinbird

The genus name comes from the Latin word *periscelis*, meaning a 'knee-bend' or 'garter'. The specific name comes from two Latin words: *tres* is the number 'three', and *color* means 'colour', or 'shade'.

In Latin America few birds have such a strange appearance. The word capuchin is reminiscent of a capuchin monk in his brown habit. Capuchin monkeys and babblers are named for the same reason. The bird's vulture-like head is covered in blue skin, and during courtship lovely orange plumes appear and flutter at the base of the tail. As the birds sing at a *lek,* they make strange chuckling and laughing sounds.

Pernis apivorus
European Honey-buzzard

Pernis was a bird of prey mentioned by Aristotle.

The specific name comes from *apis*, the Latin word for a 'bee', and *vorus*, a Latin word for 'eating'. In reality wasps are the preferred diet. As a result the honey-buzzard spends much of its time on the forest floor. The wings are therefore not adapted for long-distance flight, so migration routes over the Mediterranean use the shortest routes over water, such as the Strait of Gibraltar and the Bosphorus.

Phalacrocorax aristotelis
European Shag

The genus name comes from the Greek word *phalacros*, which means 'bald', and the Greek word *corax*, which means 'raven'. The bald prefix refers to the bare skin around the throat.

The specific name pays tribute to the Greek philosopher Aristotle, who was one of the first scientists to organise living things into groups and categories – a science called 'taxonomy'. Aristotle's work persisted for around 2,000 years until Linnaeus classified bird species in the binomial system, giving each bird a generic and a specific name, usually with a Latin or Greek etymology. The European Shag is the only bird which bears Aristotle's name.

This shag is smaller than the Great Cormorant, with a longish tail, and a small crest in the breeding season.

The plumage has a greenish sheen. It is a deep diver and finds its food on the seabed. The nest is an untidy heap of rotting seaweed and small twigs cemented by the birds' own droppings.

– P. bougainvillii
Guanay Cormorant

The species is named after Admiral L.A. de Bougainville (1729–1811), who made many expeditions to the Pacific Islands. The genus of South American flowering shrubs is also named after him.

In the islands off western South America, de Bougainville found these birds nesting in their millions, densely packed with as many as 12 birds per square metre. He discovered that the surrounding seas hold an abundance of tiny fish called anchovies, which make up the bulk of the cormorants' diet. The accumulated droppings from the Guanay Cormorant are highly prized as fertiliser. The deposit is allowed to build up over several years, then collected with shovels and pick-axes, loaded onto ships, and processed as fertilizer. For five centuries, until the time of the conquistadores, the Inca kings gathered guano as plant food.

– P. carbo
Great Cormorant

Carbo is the Latin word for 'coal'.

The English name 'cormorant' is a contraction of the Latin term *corvus marinus,* which means 'sea-crow'.

The cormorant has powerful webbed

Great Cormorant, *Phalacrocorax carbo*, drying its wings.

feet to propel it through the water, while the wings are rather short and designed to give added speed underwater. The bird pays a price, however, as typically these wings need to be held open on dry land as the bird dries out its plumage.

Fishermen in China have used the services of this cormorant since ancient times. A string attached to each bird's neck prevents the fish from being swallowed, although the string is removed to allow the bird to feed on every tenth fish.

– *P. harrisi*
Flightless Cormorant

The species name pays tribute to the philanthropist Edward Harris (1799–1863), who travelled with bird artist John James Audubon on two of his expeditions. Harris provided financial help in the production of Audubon's artistic masterpiece, *Birds of America*.

The wings of this Galápagos speciality are much reduced in size. The bird has no need to fly from predators, and the short wings have little 'drag' underwater,

Red-necked Phalarope, *Phalaropus lobatus.*

enabling the bird to fish more successfully. The bird's feathers are not waterproofed, so they are dried out between each dive.

In the past feral dogs were a huge threat in these volcanic islands, but now these have been eliminated, although any future introduction of cats and rats would undoubtedly pose a great threat.

Phalaenoptilus nuttallii
Common Poorwill

The genus name comes from two Greek words. *Phalaina* is the word for a 'moth', and *ptilon* is the word for a 'feather'.

The species name honours the botanist and ornithologist Thomas Nuttall (1786–1859).

The poorwill, unlike the majority of its nightjar cousins, does not migrate south during the winter months, but rather secretes itself among rocks, well hidden from view, with the head pointed inwards. It falls into a deep slumber, with no heart movement or breathing. This state of torpor can last for weeks or months, until the first warm rays of the spring sun. Exactly like a marmot, the poorwill's temperature falls from 40°C (104°F) to 20°C (68°F).

Phalaropus lobatus
Red-necked Phalarope

The genus name comes from two Greek words: *Phalaris* is the word for a 'coot', and *pous* means 'foot'.

The specific name is a Latin verb

meaning 'lobed'. Both the coot and the phalarope have lobed toes. In the case of the phalarope this device will enable the bird's spinning action in the water. A little whirlpool is created on the surface of the water, to bring small insects and crustaceans from below.

The female is more brightly coloured than the male, and takes the initiative during courtship. This phalarope has a northern circumpolar breeding distribution. A tagged bird in the UK on Fetlar, Shetland, travelled through Iceland and Greenland, then south through the Caribbean and Mexico, to winter at sea off Peru and Mexico, covering a distance of 25,750km (16,000 miles) in the process.

Phasianus colchicus
Common Pheasant

The genus name comes from *Phasis,* an ancient city port in Georgia, now called Poti.

The species name comes from *Colchis,* an ancient kingdom on the Black Sea which is now part of Georgia.

These were the places where Europeans first encountered this pheasant as a species introduced from Asia. Linnaeus, in searching for a description of the bird, thought its appearance so unique that only a few words need suffice: *Phasianus rufus, capite coeruleo:* 'Red Pheasant, with blue head'. He mentions its locality as Africa and Asia. Today the only pheasants in Africa are in Morocco,

although in the time of Linnaeus the species may have been more widely introduced to the coastal towns of the Mediterranean. From its origins in Asia, with the help of human introductions, the Common Pheasant has colonised much of Europe and North America, as well as parts of Australia and New Zealand.

Battle-loving Ruffs, *Philomachus pugnax.*

Philomachus pugnax
Ruff

The genus name comes from two Greek words. *Philo* means 'loving', and *mache* means 'battle'.

The species name comes from the Latin word *pugnax,* which means 'aggressive'.

The English name refers to the ornamental collar, or Ruff, which was in fashion from the 16th century.

The female is known as a Reeve. 'Ree' was an early name for the Ruff, used colloquially to mean 'frenzied'.

Phoenix from the flames: displaying Greater Flamingos, *Phoenicopterus roseus*.

There is an obvious reference to the bird's 'pumped-up' performance during the mating season. As the males compete for the attention of females in the spring, and charge into each other, they are thought to resemble fighting horsemen. The idea works better in the French language: 'Le chevalier combatant'.

Phoenicopterus roseus
Greater Flamingo

The genus name makes reference to the mythical *Phoenix*, a legendary bird which set fire to itself every 500 years, and rose from the ashes as a thing of great beauty. The Greek word *optera* means 'winged'.

The specific name comes from the Latin word for 'red'.

The red appearance is caused by the flamingo's diet. The red and blue algae they consume, along with shrimps and molluscs, contain an organic chemical loaded with beta carotene, which produces the reddish-orange pigment.

Phoenicurus phoenicurus
Common Redstart

The genus name comes from two Greek words. *Phoinix* is the word for 'red', and *ouros* means 'tailed'. *Phoinix* is associated with the legendary bird, the Phoenix, which dies in the flames so that the next generation can be born. The word is also associated with Phoenicia, a Mediterrarean state where purple dye was produced from the conch shell. The colour resembled the bird's plumage. Because dyed garments were associated with the upper classes, this was considered a 'royal' bird.

This redstart is a common European bird, which constantly quivers its red tail. 'Start' is an old name for tail.

Phylloscopus collybita
Common Chiffchaff

The genus name comes from two Greek words: *Phylum* means 'leaf', and refers to its greenish plumage. *Scopeo* is the verb 'to see'.

The genus name comes from the Latin noun *collybus*, which means the business of 'moneychanging'. There could be some confusion here with the Wood Warbler, which has a song that sounds rather like a spinning coin.

In English the bird is named onomatopoeically for its song, which is a simple *chiff-chaff* endlessly repeated.

The primary feathers of the chiffchaff are slightly shorter than those of the Willow Warbler, and the bird's migration journey to southern Europe and North Africa is shorter than that of its close relative.

– P. proregulus
Pallas's Warbler

The species name comes from the Latin word *regulus*, meaning a 'little king', and this gem-like bird has golden stripes on its crown.

The Pallas's Warbler is a tiny bird

which breeds in Siberia. It had never been seen in Britain until a specimen was shot in 1896 at Cley-next-the-Sea, Norfolk, in the days when the adage 'What's hit is history, what's missed is mystery' meant that the presentation of a skin was essential for acceptance into the record books. These days the Pallas's Warbler is seen in Britain in small numbers each year, and the increasing records of this species and other migrants from the east perhaps suggests that these are scouting parties prospecting for suitable breeding places in the future.

– P. trochilus
Willow Warbler

The genus name is uncertain. *Trochaeus* is a Latin word for a metrical term, *trochee*, which describes a metrical foot with one long and one short syllable. Alternatively, the *hoo-eet* call note of the bird could easily be transcribed as a '*trochee*'.

The Willow Warbler breeds in much of Europe and northern Asia, and winters in Sub-Saharan Africa. The song is a lovely liquid cascade, rising in volume. The dome-shaped nest is built close to the ground.

Pica pica
Eurasian Magpie

The word *Pica* is a derivative of the word piebald, meaning 'black and white'. Country folk may refer to the bird simply as 'the pie'.

This magpie has a keen eye for any

The Eurasian Magpie, *Pica pica*, has a reputation as a collector.

shiny object that could adorn its nest. It can't, however, differentiate between gold sovereigns and shiny paper. Abandoned nests may just as easily turn up a wedding ring as a sweet wrapper. Its appetite for food is similar, and pica is also the name for a condition in humans where non-nutritive items are eaten, including earth, hair, paper, and so on.

Picathartes oreas
Grey-necked Picathartes

The genus name is a joining of two words. *Pica* is the Latin word for a

Magpie, and *kathartes* comes from the Greek word for pure. So *kathartes* means the purifier, and is also the genus name for some species of American vultures. The 'magpie-vulture' seems an ugly name for such an iconic species.

The picathartes is one of the most desirable sightings for birdwatchers visiting West Africa, where the bird is considered to be sacred, and is also a symbol for ecotourism. The 'rockfowl', another name for the bird, has also appeared on numerous postage stamps.

Picus viridis
Green Woodpecker

The genus name comes from the Greek word *picos*, which means 'woodpecker', and the Latin word *viridis*, which means 'green'.

Among country folk the name 'yaffle' is used, and refers to the call of the bird, which resembles hysterical laughter.

The Green Woodpecker drums rarely, and spends most of its time on the ground licking up ants with its long tongue, which is 10cm (4in) long and wound around the skull when retracted. The salivary gland contains a sticky substance to hold the prey in place.

Heavy and prolonged snowfall will hamper the bird's ability to feed and the mortality rate can be high, but the

The 'yaffle' having the last laugh – the tree canopy keeps the woodpeckers dry, while the golfers struggle in the wet weather underneath.

Green Woodpecker revels in the rain, and has enjoyed the name 'rainbird' among country folks. Its preferred habitat of mixed woodland makes golf courses a hot favourite.

Pinguinus impennis
Great Auk

The word *pinguinnis* means 'penguin' and has an uncertain etymology. It has been suggested that it comes from two Welsh words: *Pen* meaning 'head', and *gwyn* meaning 'white'.

The species name comes from the Latin word '*pennis*', meaning 'wing', while the prefix *im* gives the meaning 'flightless'.

Pitohui dichrous
Hooded Pitohui

The genus name describes the song, and the species name '*dichoreus*' is a Latin word meaning 'double-trochee'. Trochee is a metrical foot of two syllables, the first long and the second short. In other words the song can be rendered in metrical terms as 'long-short, long-short'.

Last of their Kind

The flightless Great Auk bred on isolated rocky islands where fish were plentiful. It played an important part in prehistoric cultures in North America, where graves have been found containing its bones and skulls. Its height at 84cm (33in) gave it a near-mythical status.

Great Auk, *Pinguinus impennis*.

Early explorers hunted the Great Auk for food, or as bait for fishing, and its clumsy appearance on land meant it was easy prey. Moreover the demand for its feathery down helped to hasten its end. As it became rarer, museums and private collections were keen to acquire eggs and skins.

In 1840 a Great Auk was killed on the island of St Kilda, UK, in the belief that it was a witch responsible for a great storm. In 1844 the last two known birds were killed on the island of Eldey, off Iceland, and their skins sold to a dealer.

A blogger recently wrote of his success in cloning Great Auk genetic material with the Razorbill, and producing a perfect facsimile. The science in the article seemed plausible, but the date gave it away: 1st April 2016.

The Hooded Pitohui lives in Papua New Guinea, and it looks rather like an oriole. Researchers studying birds-of-paradise found that they felt numbness and irritation in their hands after handling the pitahuis in nets. It was discovered that the birds' feathers and skin contain the same toxin found in poison dart frogs in Amazonia (where human hunters also use it on the tips of their blow darts). The birds were getting their poison from a diet of *Choresine* beetles, and the build up of toxins in the bird offered it protection against predators such as hawks and snakes.

Platalea leucorodia
Eurasian Spoonbill

The genus name comes from the Latin word for 'flat', referring to the shape of the bill.

The species name is derived from two Latin words and means 'clothed in white'.

Ploceus velatus
Southern Masked Weaver

The scientific name comes from two Latin words. The verb *plico*, which means 'to fold together', and the noun *velamen*, meaning a 'veil'.

The Southern Masked Weaver is known for its intricately knitted nest. Inside the young are raised in almost total darkness. To help the adults pinpoint their exact position in the nest, the young have bright orange or yellow edges to their beaks. These shine intensely in the dark, and act as signals to bring food unerringly to their mouths.

Each species of weaver has a different building technique, and some species

Record Maker

The European Golden Plover was instrumental in the creation of the *Guinness Book of Records*. A shooting party in Ireland where Sir Hugh Beaver (1890–1967), the head of Guinness Breweries, was present debated whether the Red Grouse or the golden plover was the fastest in flight.

Sir Hugh had heard of the McWhirter twins, Norris and Ross, who had set up a fact-finding agency in London. He commissioned them to write a book on the sort of subjects hotly debated in pubs and clubs and private homes: who, what or which, was the fastest, the slowest, highest, longest, best at any sport you care to mention, and so on. He had tested their knowledge with a simple question; Which European language had the most irregular verbs? They had answered immediately that it was Turkish.

The *Guinness Book of Records* was born on 27th August 1955 and became a bestseller immediately. And the answer to the question which started the whole enterprise: the golden plover was the fastest-flying European gamebird.

have nests with several compartments, while entry can be from above, below or through the side. Hanging nests offer the best defence against predators such as tree snakes.

Pluvialis apricaria
European Golden Plover

The genus name comes from a Latin word *pluvia* meaning 'rain'. The adjective *pluvialis* means 'pertaining to rain'.

The species name comes from the Latin verb *apricor*, which means 'to bask in the sun', and refers to the golden upperparts.

– P. dominica
American Golden Plover

The species name is geographical and refers to Santo Domingo, a former name for Hispaniola.

The American and Pacific Golden Plovers were previously considered as one species, and named 'Lesser Golden Plover', but now they have been 'split'.

The American Golden Plover breeds in the Arctic tundra, and winters in southern South America. In spring the birds migrate overland, but they take a different route in fall when the journey is down the western side of the Atlantic and over the Caribbean, a total of 25,000km (15,500 miles). Of this, around 2,400km (1,500 miles) is over open sea, where the bird cannot feed or drink. Before migration the bird stocks up on food to produce body fat for the journey.

Egyptian Plover, *Pluvianus aegyptius*.

– P. fulva
Pacific Golden Plover

The species name comes from the Latin word *fulva*, meaning 'tawny-coloured'. This species is smaller, slimmer and longer-legged than the European Golden Plover, and the wing feathers fold beyond the tail.

Scientists have fitted them with geolocators, which showed that they can fly 4,800km (3,000 miles) from Alaska to Hawaii in 3–4 days.

Pluvianus aegyptius
Egyptian Plover

The genus name comes from the Latin word, *pluvia*, which means 'rain'. *Aegyptius* is a geographical term for 'Egypt'.

In the 4th century BC the Greek writer Herodotus wrote that Nile Crocodiles opened their mouths wide so that a bird called '*trochilus*' could fly inside their jaws and pick their teeth clean. Many people thought that this was a reference to the Egyptian Plover, hence

Takahe, *Porphyrio hochstetteri*, on a predator-free island in New Zealand.

accounts by Herodotus are suspect and dependant on hearsay.

Whatever the case, the Egyptian Plover is a beautiful bird that is often very tame. The eggs are laid in the sand and covered over for 'mother nature' to incubate. Parents will cool the nest site with water from their breasts, and the chicks may be partially buried in times of danger.

Porphyrio hochstetteri
South Island Takahe

The genus name comes from a Latin word *Porphyreticus,* which means 'purple-red'. Hochstetter (1829–1884) was a geologist commissioned by the New Zealand government to make a survey of the islands.

In 1898 the takahe was declared extinct. Then in 1948 a small population was found on the shores of Lake Orbell, a stretch of water in a highly mountainous region. Later two further groups were found, in grassland in the Musgrave and Kepler ranges. These are jealously guarded and birds have been transferred to a number of predator-free offshore islands, including some where the public can watch them.

Porzana pusilla
Baillon's Crake

The genus name was a term used by Venetians to describe a small rail.

The species name is the Latin word for 'very small'.

The English name pays homage to Louis Baillon (1778–1855), a French naturalist who developed a collection of bird skins that had been started by his father, which eventually grew to 6,000 specimens. Many were species seen by Europeans for the first time, from voyages of exploration as far afield as Oceania and South America.

Prosiciger aterrimus
Palm Cockatoo

The genus name comes from two Latin words. *Proboscis* originally meant the 'trunk of an elephant', and *gerere* was the verb 'to carry'. *Prosciger* is an apt name, as the powerful bill, as large as its head, can crack open the most obdurate of nuts, and break off branches for its 'drumming display'. This is a courtship ritual where a stick is knocked against the hollow of a tree. The male thus demonstrates to the female that he owns this hollow, this piece of real estate. If she will only come closer to inspect the depth and lining, the comfort and solidity of the structure, she will be convinced he can provide for her.

The remarkable crest of the Palm Cockatoo, *Probosciger aterrimus*.

The specific name comes from the Latin word *ater*, meaning 'black', and is the superlative form, meaning very black.

The Palm Cockatoo is a bird of northern Australia and Papua New Guinea, much prized in the pet trade because of its unusual appearance. It has pinkish cheek patches which become brighter, and appear to 'blush', when the bird is agitated or aroused.

Psarisomus dalhousiae
Long-tailed Broadbill

It is difficult to study the etymology of the Long-tailed Broadbill without being 'wreathed in smiles', for that is exactly the meaning of the genus name. *Psao* comes from the future tense of the Greek verb 'to see', and *risor* is the Latin word for 'someone who mocks'. With its wide gape, the bird does seem to be laughing at the observer.

The species name honours Christian Ramsay (1786–1839), the Countess of Dalhousie, who was a botanical collector of specimens from locations including Canada and India.

These are lovely forest birds, easily seen at locations such as Doi Suthep or Doi Inthanon in Thailand.

Pseudochelidon sirintarae
White-eyed River Martin

The genus name comes from two Greek words, meaning 'false swallow', emphasising its distinctness from 'true' swallows.

The species is named after the Thai princess Sirindhorn, a daughter of King Bhumibol Adulyadej, for her keen interest in natural history.

A pair of 'happy looking' Long-tailed Broadbills, *Psarisomus dalhousiae*.

An ornithologist found villagers at Boraphet, Thailand, were selling these birds, either to be released from cages by monks to obtain good 'karma', or for eating. They have been well photographed in the hand, but there are no firm sightings since 1980. The bird's large eyes suggest a crepuscular or nocturnal species.

Psittacula krameri
Ring-necked Parakeet

The genus name is the diminutive form of the Latin word *psittacus*, which means 'parrot'. W.H. Kramer (died 1765) was a German naturalist.

There is a long history of caged parakeets in ancient Greece and Rome. The attraction was their ability to mimic human speech. As an introduced species they have now colonised large parts of Europe, for example certain London parks hold roosts of several thousand birds. The birds have adapted well to city living, and can withstand the cold of northern winters.

Psittacus erithacus
African Grey Parrot

The genus name is the Latin word for a parrot, and the species name was used by Aristotle to refer to an unknown bird.

The African Grey Parrot is commonly kept in captivity as a 'companion parrot' due to an ability to remember large sections of the human repertoire: numbers, lines of poetry, swear words (of whose meaning it is entirely innocent!)

and pithy comments are all stored within its head.

Because of their ability to interact with humans, they are harvested on a huge scale throughout countries in Central Africa to be used as household pets. Around 20 per cent of the wild population is taken every year, and many die in transit to human ownership. The collecting of wild birds is now illegal, but the practice is hard to stop among poor communities for whom the cagebird trade can be so profitable.

Because these parrots are highly intelligent they need constant stimulation. If bored they become easily distressed and will self-harm through feather-plucking.

Pternistis ochropectus
Djibouti Francolin

Pterux is the Greek word for 'wing'.

The species name comes from the Greek word *ochro,* meaning 'yellow', and the Latin word *pectus*, meaning 'breast'.

This gamebird is endemic to Djibouti and is a classic example of a bird approaching extinction due to habitat degradation. Once common, and eaten in good numbers as it lived in close proximity to humans, the bird is now listed as Critically Endangered and has retreated to high ground. In the past ten years only one nest has been found.

Pterodroma cahow
Bermuda Petrel

The genus name comes from two Greek

words: *pterux* means 'wing', and *dromas* means 'running' or 'moving quickly'.

The specific name refers to the bird's call, an eerie sound which frightened sailors.

When Spanish conquistadores used Bermuda as a stepping-stone for the plunder of the Incas, they harvested huge numbers of 'Cahow' – up to 400 per night – as food. Pigs were taken to the island by ship to feed the sailors, and these rooted in the petrel burrows to eat eggs, chicks and adults. Rats, cats and dogs continued the killing and by 1620, only 10 years later, there were no more sightings.

Following a hiatus of more than 300 years, in 1951 a young boy of 15 was present when 18 pairs of Bermuda Petrels were found nesting in the rocky outcrops of Castle Harbour. The young lad, David Wingate, made it his life's ambition to conserve the species. As an adult he invented a wooden baffle which allowed the petrel access to its burrow, but was too large for the predatory White-tailed Tropicbirds. He also arranged for the reforestation of Nonsuch Island, off the Bermuda coast, as petrel breeding habitat, while artificial concrete bunkers and plastic boxes provided nesting holes. Most inventive was installing a sound system on the island, aimed at winning back these birds by playing recordings of their nocturnal mating calls!

The population seems to be on a slow upward trend so a vanished bird, Lazarus-like, has come back from the grave.

Pteroglossus bitorquatus
Red-necked Araçari

The genus name comes from the Greek word *pterux,* which means 'wing', and the word *glossy,* which seems to have a Scandinavian origin, and means 'shiny'.

The specific name comes from two Latin words. *Bis* means 'twice', and *torquatus* means 'turned', referring to the red and yellow bands on the breast.

A Rare Encounter

The 'Foret du Jour', where the Djibouti Francolin lived in good numbers, is now a dead forest. Whitened branches and tree stumps poke from the earth. Years of drought and soil erosion have forced the birds elsewhere. Juniper has given way to box trees, and goats wander freely and eat whatever they can find.

The author recalls a climb with a local ornithologist at a nearby site, arriving at an altitude of 1,060m (3,500ft). Basalt rocks had to be negotiated in total silence, and then three Djibouti Francolin appeared, as if in instalments. Through the scrub a head appeared, then a short tail, then the rusty flanks, and finally green feet with wicked-looking spurs. These will help the male to defend his territory from rivals.

The araçaris are a group of gaudily coloured, small, and slender toucans from Central America. They nest in tree hollows, and will shelter there at night. To fit into these cavities they must 'fold' themselves by turning the bill over the back, then folding the tail feathers over the bill. That way they take up only a third of their normal space. Up to five adults and their offspring can share a home for the night.

Satin Bowerbird, *Ptilonorhynchus violaceus*, at the bower.

Ptilonorhynchus violaceus
Satin Bowerbird

The genus comes from *ptilon*, the Greek word for 'feather', and *rhynchos*, the Greek word for 'beak'. There are downy feathers which cover part of the upper mandible.

The species name describes the violet appearance of the male's plumage and the birds' eyes. Bowerbirds, as the name suggests, construct elaborate specialised stick structures called bowers, which they decorate with shiny objects including plastic items, flowers and berries. The Satin Bowerbird prefers items which are blue in colour.

The females visit throughout the construction process, and make their choice from a variety of 'building sites'. It seems that younger females will choose to mate with a male whose house building is elaborate, while older females will choose a partner with a more complex courtship dance. Once mating is over, the male leaves the female to raise the young in the bower of her choice.

Puffinus puffinus
Manx Shearwater

The scientific name comes from a description of the carcasses of young birds prepared for the table. They are neatly packaged and appear 'swollen' or 'puffed-out'. These chicks are large and rich in oil, and are still eaten in the Faroe Islands.

The English name makes reference to the Isle of Man, where the species used to breed until the colony was wiped out by rats from a shipwreck.

Manx Shearwaters have a strong homing instinct, and can return to their burrows even when released from hundreds of miles distant. Their sense of smell is acute, and they can detect offal from tens of kilometres away.

Pycnonotus jucundus
Red-whiskered Bulbul

The genus name comes from *pyknos*, a Greek word meaning 'bold', and '*notus*', a Latin word meaning 'known as', or 'notorious'.

Singing Red-whiskered Bulbul, *Pycnonotus jucundus*.

The species name comes from *iocundus*, the Latin word for 'cheerful'.

The scientific name well explains the bird's popularity as a cagebird. The Red-whiskered Bulbul interacts well with humans, and will entertain with its song throughout the day. The song, indeed, has been transcribed as 'pleased to meet you'.

Pyrrhocorax pyrrhocorax
Red-billed Chough

Pyr is the Greek word for 'fire', and *corax* is the Latin word for a 'raven'. The legs and bill are fiery red.

The English name is an example of onomatopoeia. 'Chough' is exactly the call of this bird of rocky mountains and cliffs.

These are mountain specialists that have nested at altitudes of 6,500m (21,300ft), which is higher than any other bird species, while birds have been seen following mountaineers on Mount Everest at a height of 8,200m (26,900ft).

– P. graculus
Alpine Chough

The species name comes from the Latin word for a jackdaw.

This is a high-altitude species that is often visible around tourist sites, especially ski slopes.

The Alpine Chough is more vocal than its Red-billed relative, uttering whistling sounds and gentle warbles.

Rallus aquaticus
Water Rail

The genus name comes from *rallus*, the Latin word for 'thin'. The body is laterally compressed, to enable the bird to slip easily through dense vegetation.

The species name is the Latin word for 'living by the water'. The Water Rail is a skulker and likes to stay well hidden, but will sometimes appear in the open, especially during severe weather. The species was considered a delicacy by the Romans, and is featured in wall-paintings at Pompeii.

Ramphastos toco
Toco Toucan

The genus name comes from *ramus*, the Latin word for a branch, and *fastus*, the Latinised form of the Greek word for 'haughty'.

The genus name suits the regal appearance of this bird, which is the largest member of the toucan family. Amerindian tribes believed the Toco Tocan was a conduit between humans and the spirit world.

The specific name is a form of *tukana*, a Portuguese variant of the name given to the bird by the Tupi people.

This lovely 'art nouveau' painting of Toco Toucan, *Ramphastos toco*, shows features including the huge colourful bill, bright plumage, and the sheer charisma of these birds.

Raphus cucullatus
Dodo

The genus name makes reference to the bustards, which the Dodo was thought to resemble. *Cucullus* is the Latin name for 'hood', and refers to the hooded appearance of the Dodo's head.

The only full skeleton of the bird can be seen in the Natural History Museum on the island of Mauritius. The first humans to cast eyes on these flightless creatures were Portuguese sailors who landed in 1598. As the birds had never been in contact with humans they were fearless and thought to be stupid.

The English name has several possible origins. One is the Dutch word *dodaars*, meaning 'knot-arse', which makes reference to the knot feathers on the hind leg. Another possible origin is the Portuguese word *doudo*, meaning 'fool'.

The Dodo stood 0.9m (3ft) high and weighed around 20kg (45lb), so made for an easy meal. Within a hundred years they had fallen prey to human greed, and to the animals the sailors brought with them, such as cats, dogs, rats and monkeys.

Dodo, *Raphus cucullatus*.

Recurvirostra avosetta
Pied Avocet

The genus name comes from *recurvus*, the Latin word for 'curved backwards', and 'rostrum', the Latin for a 'beak'. The bill curves upwards and sweeps through the water from side to side.

The species name comes from an Italian word for a 'lawyer'. In its handsome black and white livery, the bird resembles a French lawyer or Advocate (L'Avocat). This is an aggressive species which likes to keep the feeding space all to itself. Spare a thought for any tiny wader which comes too close – it may be served with a writ!

The name Pied Avocet, *Recurvirostra avosetta*, has its origins in the legal profession.

Regulus regulus
Goldcrest

Regulus is a diminutive form of the Latin word *rex*, which means 'king'. The Goldcrest is literally a 'kinglet'. At 8.4cm (3.3in) in length, this is the smallest of all the European birds. It weighs about the same as a British five-pence piece. Despite their apparent fragility, these are hardy birds which can survive the winter north of the Arctic Circle in Norway.

Remiz pendulinus
Eurasian Penduline-tit

Remiz is the Polish name for the penduline-tit, and *pendulus* is the Latin word for 'hanging down' or 'suspended'. The nest is an intricate hanging structure, which in the past was reputedly sturdy enough to form the basis of a child's shoe in poorer parts of central Europe.

Rhinoplax vigil
Helmeted Hornbill

The genus name comes from *rhynchos*, the Greek word for nose, and *plasticos*, from *plassein*, the Greek verb 'to shape'.

The species name is the Latin for 'watchful' or 'awake'.

Unlike other hornbill species, the casque of the Helmeted Hornbill is solid, and is used by males as a weapon in head-to-head combat. The ivory has a lovely golden-yellow colour, is silky to the touch, and is considered a valuable carving material. Large numbers of these

The Critically Endangered Helmeted Hornbill, *Rhinoplax vigil*.

birds are killed each year for their casques. While the ivory trade in elephants and rhinos is well known, this trade tends to slip under the radar. Hornbill ivory sells for around US$6,000 per kilo, three times the cost of rhino or elephant ivory. The ivory trade is organised by criminal gangs, and much of the ivory is shipped to China.

Numbers of Helmeted Hornbills are lost each year due to habitat destruction, as lowland forest is felled in Borneo and Sumatra to satisfy the western appetite for palm oil.

The slow reproductive rate of these birds makes it hard to increase population size, as a single fledgling is produced each year. The female is walled up in the nest for 160 days during incubation. If the male is killed, she may be in moult and unable to fly, and will lose her life along with the chick.

Rupicola rupicola
Guianan Cock-of-the-Rock

The scientific name comes from two Latin words: *Rupes* means 'cliff', and *collere* is the verb 'to dwell'.

A 19th century engraving of the Guianan Cock-of-the-Rock, *Rupicola rupicola*.

A Lazy Lover

Males are bright orange and gather in 'leks' of around 50 birds. They display their crests and secondary feathers to advantage, and once a female has made her choice, she flies down to the ground and pecks the male on the rump. For all his beauty and posturing, his work ceases with the act of copulation. The female builds the nest, incubates the eggs, and raises the young entirely alone. The male starts all over again: preening, swaggering and showing his best side.

Rynchops flavirostris
African Skimmer

The genus name comes from *rhynchos*, the Greek word for a 'nose' or 'beak'.

The specific name comes from two Latin words: *flavus* means 'reddish-yellow' and *rostrum* means 'beak'.

Skimmers feed by flying low, and dipping their lower mandibles into the

Feeding Black Skimmer, *Rynchops niger*.

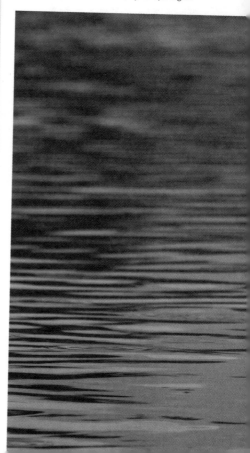

water. When the bird makes contact with a fish, the bill snaps shut. The unique bill-structure enables this method of fishing, as the lower mandible is much longer than the upper.

This skimmer is a bird of Sub-Saharan Africa. It migrates on a north to south axis, following the rainy seasons when fish are abundant.

– *R. niger*
Black Skimmer

This is a bird of North and South America, whose specific name is the Latin word for 'black'.

As above, this is another tern-like species, with a buoyant and graceful flight. The lower mandible skims the surface of the water for food. The birds feed by touch, and the whole colony on a sandbank may disappear at dark to feed collectively.

Sagittarius serpentarius
Secretarybird

The genus name is the Latin word for an 'archer'.

The specific name refers to the bird's preferred diet of snakes.

The English name refers to the 'quills' at the rear of the nape, which are not unlike a pen lodged behind a writer's ear.

With its long legs the Secretarybird prefers walking and running on the ground to catch prey. It can kill snakes by stamping repeatedly on their heads, and may swallow them whole. Prey is flushed from the grass by stamping on the surrounding vegetation.

Snakes, lizards and other prey can slither, run, scuttle or hide, but once the Secretarybird attacks, its success rate is close to 100 per cent. They are often seen near fires, waiting to devour any escapees.

The Secretarybird, *Sagittarius serpentarius*, specialises in feeding on snakes.

Saxicola rubicola
European Stonechat

The genus name comes from two Latin words: *saxum* means 'rock', and *incolla* means 'inhabitant'.

The species name is derived from two Latin words: *rubus* means 'bramble bush', and *incolla* means 'inhabitant'.

The English name refers to the call-note, which sounds like stones clicking together.

With stonechats the birding community divides into 'splitters' and 'lumpers' – below are two forms which are treated by some as full species and by others as subspecies.

– *S. maurus*
Siberian Stonechat

Maurus comes from the Greek word *mauros*, meaning 'black', making reference to the colour of the upperparts.

– *S. torquatus*
African Stonechat

The species name is a Latin word meaning 'collared'.

Scolopax minor
American Woodcock

The genus name is Latin for a number of similar bird species and families, especially the snipe.

The species name is Latin, and refers to its small size.

The plumage of this species is a cryptic mix of grey, black and brown to avoid detection. Nevertheless around half a million are shot yearly by hunters. The tip of the upper mandible is flexible, and can open and shut underground when the long bill is probing for food.

A male American Woodcock, *Scolopax minor*, strutting his stuff in the twilight.

The long tongue is rough in texture to grasp slippery prey.

Viewers use the term 'sky-dance' to describe the mating display of the male. A nasal 'cheep' is the cue for action as the bird spirals upwards, then tumbles out of the sky like a stricken aircraft. A soft liquid warble gives notice he is about to land, then he planes off, touches base, and starts again. The male's ground moves resemble some of the best disco-dancing.

Yes, *Scolopax minor* is worth a long wait in the dusk.

– *S. rusticola*
Eurasian Woodcock

Rusticola is a Latin word for 'countryman'.

The species has a rotund body shape, cryptic brown and buff markings as camouflage, and a long slender bill. It is best known for its 'roding' display, when the male flies with fast jerky wing-beats at dusk, calling out with sounds reminiscent of the croak of a frog and the song of a cricket.

Serinus serinus
European Serin

Serin is the French word for a canary, probably from the Latin word *citrinus*, which means 'yellow'.

The serin could easily be confused with a similar small seed-eating finch, the Eurasian Siskin. The siskin, however, appears predominately green in colour, while the serin is lemon-coloured and heavily streaked.

– S. canaria
Island Canary

The species name is geographical and refers to the Canary Islands. Some say that the islands were named after the dogs (in Latin, *canarii*) found there, or possibly after seals, which were sometimes known as 'sea dogs'.

Well into the 20th century, coal miners took caged canaries into the pit as an early warning system to detect the presence of carbon monoxide. These delicate birds become sick at the slightest presence of toxic gases, and gave the miners time to escape.

Canaries are kept as household pets, and selective breeding has produced many domestic varieties and wonderful singers.

Somateria mollissima
Common Eider

The genus name comes from two Greek words: *Soma* means 'body', and *erion* means 'wool'.

The specific name is the Latin word for 'very soft'.

Eiderdown comes from the breasts of adult females, who pluck it from their bellies during the nesting season to adorn the nest and cover the eggs. The soft underbelly then becomes the brood-patch.

The strands are finer than human hair, and have a unique ability to conserve heat and provide comfort. In Iceland eiders often seek to nest near human populations for protection. Harvesters of down will help to protect nesting birds from predators such as foxes, ravens and gulls. The down has to be meticulously washed and prepared in order to rid it of straw, moss and seaweed.

Steatornis caripensis
Oilbird

The genus name comes from two Latin words meaning 'fat bird', and refers to the young nestlings.

Caripe is a geographical term referring to Caripe in Venezuela, where Alexander von Humboldt (1769–1859) first studied the bird.

Flocks of Oilbirds leave their caves to feed at night, often travelling long distances and using their excellent sense of smell to find aromatic fruiting trees. They pluck the fruit while still in flight, store it in their stomachs, and digest it during the day when they have returned to roost in their caves.

In the blackness of the cave, they find their way using echolocation. For the Oilbird, light is the enemy. When human visitors are guided to the caves, the leader will only allow the faintest of flashlights, otherwise the birds become very stressed.

Young birds are fed large quantities of fruit before they fly, and can be much larger than the adults. In the past chicks were captured and boiled down to make oil, hence the name Oilbird.

Stercorarius parasiticus
Arctic Skua or Parasitic Jaeger

Stercorarius is the Latin word for 'dung'. It was once thought that their food, disgorged by birds who were robbed, was excrement.

Parasiticus reflects the piratical habits of these birds, which steal food from other seabirds such as terns.

Sterna dougallii
Roseate Tern

The use of the word *Sterna* (*stearn*) for a tern originates from the 10th century poem 'The Seafarer', in which a sailor describes the desolate hardships of a life at sea: a life of loneliness, cold and hunger, whereas men on land have their kinsmen for company, with food and wine to drink.

Then the writer realises that life on land is no better, with its empty pleasures. The last few verses consider that the afterlife will reveal the perfect state. Some authors think the last verses were added later, and the poem has no allegorical

purpose. Whatever the case, Linnaeus used the word *sterna* for a genus of seabirds noted for their long migrations.

The specific name is given in memory of the ornithologist Dr Peter McDougall (1777–1814), an explorer and collector.

'Roseate' refers to the rosy tinge on the breast.

Like other members of the genus, the Roseate Tern feeds by plunge-diving into the sea, preferring to fish in seawater rather than freshwater lagoons.

The Roseate Tern is a 'kleptoparasite', and will steal from other birds, especially puffins. This is partly a survival strategy, as sometimes bad weather drives fish down to depths that only the puffin and other auks can reach.

– S. hirundo
Common Tern

The specific name is the Latin word for a 'swallow' making reference to the similar slender build and forked tail. The bird nests in the Northern Hemisphere and migrates to West Africa. A colloquial name for this bird is the 'sea swallow'.

– S. paradisaea
Arctic Tern

Paradisaea originates from a Greek word, *paradeisos*, which comes from the Persian word for a 'garden'. The word makes reference to the lovely, other-worldly appearance of the tern. *Paradisus* is the Latin word for 'heaven'.

Arctic Tern, *Sterna paradisaea* – the greatest migrant of all.

Recently the annual migration of one Arctic Tern was measured at 90,000km (56,000 miles) for the round trip, from Northumberland, UK, to the Antarctic and back. A tiny geolocator the size of a small sweet was attached to the bird's leg, and recorded every wing-beat of that epic journey.

Streptopelia decaocto
Collared Dove

The genus and species names are entirely based on Greek. *Strepto* means 'collar', and *peleia* means 'dove'. *Decaocto* is the Greek number 18. *Deca* means 10, and *octo* means 8.

In Greek mythology, the story is told of a young servant girl whose yearly salary is 18 drachma. When she complains at the paltry sum, the gods turn her into a dove, whose mournful cries reflect her sadness.

– S. turtur
Turtle Dove

For hundreds of years the soporific purr has given the bird its name: *Turtur* in Latin, *Tourterelle* in French, *Turteltaube* in German. This lovely bird, so symbolic of high summer and warm afternoons, may soon be extinct as a breeding bird in the UK. This will happen despite the bird's reputation for fidelity. In Shakespeare's play *The Winter's Tale*, for example,

Florizel leads Perdita to the dance with the words, 'Your hand, my Perdita, as turtles pair, that never mean to part'.

The Turtle Dove's departure is blamed on modern forms of intensive agriculture. More telling is the huge toll taken every year by hunters, especially in places such as Malta, where the tradition of killing birds is so hard to eradicate.

Strigops habroptilus
Kakapo

The genus name comes from two Greek words. *Stryx is* the word for an 'owl', and *ops* comes from the verb, 'to see'. The bird, literally, looks like an owl.

The species name comes from two Greek words. *Habros* means 'soft', and *ptilon* means 'feather'.

The English name is derived from the Maori *kaka* meaning 'parrot', and *po* meaning 'night'.

Each foot has two forward- and two backward-pointing toes, enabling the bird to climb trees with ease. Kakapo were formerly hunted by the Maori for food, and their skins and feathers used for making cloaks.

When weasels and stoats were released in New Zealand to control the rabbit population, the numbers of Kakapo fell disastrously. There were attempts to place them on remote islands for safety, but predators were able to gain access and further reduced numbers. The Kakapo is listed as Critically Endangered, with only around 120 living individuals.

These are closely monitored and each is given a name.

Strix aluco
Tawny Owl

The binomial name comes from the Greek word *strix*, meaning 'owl', and the Latin verb *ululo*, meaning 'to screech'.

To enable the bird to hunt successfully at night, the ears are elliptical. The sound of a mouse rustling in the grass arrives at each ear at a different interval of time. These 'co-ordinates' enable the Tawny Owl to pinpoint its prey with great accuracy. Strangely, the sound of raindrops interferes with this ability. During prolonged wet spells owls have been known to starve.

For pioneering bird photographer Eric Hosking (1909-1991), the challenge of capturing the Tawny Owl on film in 1937 could not take advantage of modern lenses and equipment. After climbing up a tree, and a close encounter beside the nest, the bird struck him in the face, resulting in the loss of an eye.

His autobiography tells the story. *An Eye for a Bird* was written in 1970, without any bitterness, and became a bestseller. Eric Hosking captured his beloved birds in black and white, setting the highest standards at the time.

Struthio camelus
Common Ostrich

The genus name *Struthio* is the Latin word for 'ostrich'.

Three of the twelve Apostlebirds, *Struthidea cinerea*.

The specific name is derived from *camera*, a Latin word for a 'vault' or 'arch', with obvious reference to the camel's hump.

This flightless bird is the world's largest, standing 2.7m (9ft) tall, and weighing up to 135kg (300lb). It lives on the African plains, among dangerous predators, and its powerful feet and legs are needed in order to run for its life.

Struthidea cinerea
Apostlebird

The genus name is derived from the Greek *strouthos*, meaning 'bird'.

The specific name comes from the Latin word *cinera,* meaning 'ashes', and refers to the bird's overall grey colouring.

The birds travel in groups of around 12, so they are named after the biblical apostles, the 12 followers of Jesus Christ.

Their gregarious nature and harsh grating notes have led to other colloquial names, including 'happy jack', 'happy families' and 'CWAs'. The last name is derogatory, referring to the 'supposed' constant chatter of the Country Women's Association. 'Lousy jack' is another name, due to their heavy louse infestations.

The birds are highly social, and live in loose associations with only one breeding pair. The others, in human terms, are aunts, uncles, cousins and unrelated adults.

Sturnus roseus
Rose-coloured Starling
Sturnus is the Latin word for 'starling'.

Roseus speaks for itself: pink plumage.

An alternative English name is Rosy Pastor, perhaps suggesting a pastor addressing his congregation at a wedding, and blushing red as he forgets the bride's name!

Sturnus vulgaris, Common Starling

– S. vulgaris
Common Starling
Vulgaris is the Latin word for 'common'.

Visitors to Times Square in New York may wonder why the place is alive with starlings. Here they chatter away with their slightly metallic songs. With their gift for mimicry, perhaps that is bird-speak for 'have a nice day'.

Around 100 birds were released by the American Acclimatisation Society, whose chairman suggested each bird mentioned by William Shakespeare should be given a chance to settle across the Atlantic. These birds would make immigrants from Britain feel at home. Among attempted introductions birds such as the Bullfinch failed to survive, but the starlings now number in their millions and have displaced various American species by taking over their nesting sites.

Sylvia atricapilla
Blackcap
The genus name comes from *silva*, the Latin word for a 'wood' or 'copse'. The species name comes from two Latin words. *Ater* means black, and *caput* means head.

The song is a rich musical warbling, leading to the moniker, the 'mock nightingale'. In Messiaen's Opera, 'Saint Francois d'Assise', the song of the Blackcap is represented when St Francis speaks to the birds. The Garden Warbler has a similar song, and opinion is divided as to the better musician.

Synthliboramphus antiquus
Ancient Murrelet
The genus name comes from *synthlibo*, the Greek verb 'to compress' or 'to synthesise', and *rhamphos*, the Greek word for 'bill'.

The species name is the Latin word for old. The head pattern resembles the shawl worn by an old woman.

The English name comes from *murre*, a Norse word for the 'guillemot', and may refer to the call made by the Common Guillemot.

The Ancient Murrelet spends more time at sea than any other bird. The chicks are taken to the water within two days of hatching, and are fed at sea. The whole family swims well away from land.

The appearance of a single Ancient Murrelet on Lundy Island, UK, in June 1990 was totally unexpected as the species' breeding grounds are in British Columbia and on islands in the north Pacific.

Syrrhaptes paradoxus
Pallas's Sandgrouse

The genus name comes from the Greek word *syrrhaptos*, which means 'sewn together'. The feathered toes are closely bound.

Paradoxos is the Greek word for 'strange'.

Pallas's Sandgrouse is a Central Asian species, whose dry diet of seeds requires lots of drinking water. At dawn and dusk large flocks gather at water holes. Males soak their breast feathers while drinking, and the chicks can suck the moisture upon their return to the nest.

The Last Arrival?

The Pallas's Sandgrouse is an irruptive species, and in the late 1800s and early 1900s birds were periodically forced from their Central Asian breeding grounds by late snow. Hundreds arrived in the UK, and the occasional pair even bred, for example near Elgin in 1908.

The present generation of British birders had never seen a sandgrouse, so the arrival of an individual near Loch of Hillwell, Shetland, in May 1990 was greeted with a great deal of excitement. Aircraft, taxi services and hotels did well as hundreds of birders made their way to the archipelago, and the bird obligingly remained until early June. There have been no further British records since then.

Young Little Grebes, *Tachybaptus ruficollis*, hitching a lift on an adult.

Tachybaptus dominicus
Least Grebe

The genus name comes from two Greek words: *tachus* means 'fast', and the verb *bapto* means 'to drown' or 'to sink'.

The species name is a geographical term, referring to the Caribbean island of Dominica, although the species is found in much of Central and South America.

Adults can be as small as 21cm (8.3in) in length. Because of its tiny size the Least Grebe may nest in very small stretches of water, to avoid the young being taken by fish. And to avoid predation by raptors the birds often stay well hidden in thick vegetation by the water's edge.

– T. ruficollis
Little Grebe

The species name comes from two Latin words: *Rufus* means 'red', and *collum* means 'collar'. Taking into account the genus name (see above), the Little Grebe's scientific name translates literally as 'red-collared fast-sinker'!

The bird's range extends across much of Europe, Africa and Asia. It is an excellent swimmer, and nests close to the water's edge, since the legs are set far back on the body, making it difficult to walk. The young leave the nest and can swim soon after hatching, and are often given a piggyback by the parents.

The male Red-flanked Bluetail, *Tarsiger cyanurus*, is a beautiful bird.

Tarsiger cyanurus
Red-flanked Bluetail

The genus name comes from the Greek word *tarsus*, meaning the flat of the foot, and the Latin word *gerere*, meaning 'to carry'.

The species name also comes from two Greek words. *Kuanos* means 'dark blue', and *ouros* means 'tail'.

Formerly considered a Siberian breeder, the Red-flanked Bluetail is slowly expanding its range westwards and now there are several hundred breeding pairs in Finland. It has become an increasingly regular annual autumn visitor to Britain, often appearing when there is an easterly wind and a high-pressure area over Scandinavia. Watch that weather vane.

Tetrao tetrix
Black Grouse

The Black Grouse was described by Linnaeus in his *Systema Natura* (1758), and still bears its original binomial name. *Tetrao* and *tetrix* are Ancient Greek words referring to some form of gamebird.

Males and females are often referred to be their traditional names, as 'blackcock' and 'greyhen' respectively. These folksy terms were first used by the parson-naturalist John Ray (1627–1705) in 1674. Ray classified birds and plants according to the similarities and differences which he observed, and was the first naturalist to give a biological definition of the word 'species'.

– *T. urogallus*
Western Capercaillie

The genus name is the Latin word for a 'grouse'.

The specific name is a New Latin word meaning 'mountain-cock'.

The English name comes from Scottish Gaelic. According to some writers it originates from *calliack*, meaning 'old woman', and *caber*, meaning 'who sits on the branch'. A more likely source, however, is *capul*, meaning 'wood', and *coille*, meaning 'horse'.

This is a turkey-sized bird with an impressive courtship display that reaches a crescendo with a sound that resembles the popping of a Champagne cork, and a fearsome reputation in its own territory. Visitors beware, the bill and spurs can draw blood. The Capercaillie is a bird with a strong libido, but it isn't much use as a reception committee.

Thalassarche chlororhyncos
Yellow-nosed Albatross

The etymology is entirely Greek. *Thalassa* means 'the sea', and *arche* is the word for 'beginning'. *Chloro* designates the colour 'yellow', and *rhyncos* means the 'nose'.

All the species of albatross can fly for miles over the southern oceans without flapping their wings, letting the wind and air currents do the work for them.

Imagine a drowsy British birder enjoying a bite of toast and cup of tea, wandering sleepily into the garden only to stumble across an albatross. Is

he dreaming? Is he sober? Early one morning in July 2007, a Yellow-nosed Albatross was discovered in a garden at Brean, Somerset. This was a new bird for Britain. It was released from the cliff top, and then made an overnight stop at an inland lake near Scunthorpe, Yorkshire, before appearing off the Swedish coast shortly afterwards.

Tichodroma muraria
Wallcreeper

The Wallcreeper is a bird of rocky precipices and ravines in Eurasia, usually above the tree line, although in winter it will move to lower elevations. The genus name comes from two Greek words. *Teikhos* means 'wall', and *dromos* means 'runner'.

The species name comes from *murus*, the Latin word for 'wall'.

The Wallcreeper is on every birdwatchers 'must-see' list, but it can be hard to spot as it creeps around on rocks and cliffs, constantly flicking its beautiful scarlet wings. The long slender bill is perfect for extracting spiders and insects from their cubby-holes.

Troglodytes troglodytes
Eurasian Wren

This tiny bird is named from two Greek words: *trogle* means hole, and *duein* means to enter. The wren's nest resembles a cave. Its home is round and entered from the side, and eggs can be numerous.

In populations found in the colder

Hunting the Wren

The sorry tradition of 'hunting the wren' is thankfully dying out. On St Stephen's Day, 26th December, a wren would be captured, tied to a pole, and paraded around the town by locals asking for charity. A feather would be given to each donor as a token of good luck, and eventually the wren would be buried. Today, where the tradition persists, an effigy of a wren will suffice. Normally people have a fondness for this tiny creature with its loud song and mouse-like foraging.

Shetland Wren, *Troglodytes troglodytes svetlandicus.*

climes of the North Atlantic islands, the birds look chunkier than those on the mainland and are considered to belong to different subspecies. The trinomial names are geographical and speak for themselves, for example *Troglodytes troglodytes svetlandicus, T.t. orcadensis,* and *T.t. faroensis.*

Turdoides squamiceps
Arabian Babbler

The genus name comes from *turdus,* the Latin name for a 'thrush', and *eidon,* the past tense of the Greek verb 'to see'. The bird, literally, 'looks like a thrush'.

Male American Robin, *Turdus migratorius*.

The species name comes from *squama,* the Latin word for 'scaly', and *caput,* the Latin word for a 'head'.

Arabian Babblers are intensely sociable birds, and share activities such as bathing, cleaning and feeding their young. They have been seen squabbling over which one will offer a gift to another. This has made them good subjects in the study of 'altruism' among birds. It has been suggested that these acts of apparent kindness give them status within the group.

Turdus eremita
Tristan Thrush

The genus name is the Latin word for 'thrush'.

The specific name comes from *eremos,* the Greek word for 'lonely', or *eremites,* the Greek word for 'living in the desert'. The English word 'hermit' shares the same etymology.

This thrush is an opportunistic scavenger and omnivore on the South Atlantic island of Tristan da Cunha, killing and plundering at will. It has been filmed breaking open the eggs of a Yellow-nosed Albatross, eating the eggs and chicks of the Great Shearwater, and dragging storm-petrels from their burrows and eating them. More recently they have been observed drinking blood from penguins by piercing the skin on the rump.

The presence of rats on any of the islands is a continuing problem for the bird, but these thrushes are so aggressive that we shouldn't be surprised if they found a way to add the rat to the menu.

Common Blackbird, *Turdus merula*.

– *T. merula*
Common Blackbird

Merula is the Latin name for blackbird.

The song is a melodious flute-like warble, delivered from a vantage point, which may be a chimney stack, pylon or tree top. When the bird prepares to settle for the night, a *chink-chink* series of notes are intended to deter others from sharing its sleeping quarters. When a cat is nearby, *pook-pook* notes are delivered as a warning to other birds of the predator.

In medieval times the practice of placing live birds under the crust of a pie gave rise to the song, 'Sing a Song of Sixpence'. The song speaks of 'four and twenty Blackbirds baked in a pie, when the pie was opened the birds began to sing. Wasn't that a dainty dish to set before the King'. Birds as large as swans, as well as small songbirds, would often decorate the dishes at royal banquets.

– *T. migratorius*
American Robin

Turdus is the Latin word for 'thrush', and the species name comes from the Latin word *migrage*, which means 'to go'.

The English name refers to the colour of the bird's breast, which is a similar orange-red to that of the European Robin, which belongs to a different family. The thrush was named 'robin' by homesick settlers in North America.

– *T. philomelos*
Song Thrush

The species name comes from two Greek words: *philo* means 'loving', and *melos* means 'song'. Together they make the name Philomela, a young Princess in Ovid's Greek mythology.

In the myth, Philomela is ravished by King Tereus. Her tongue is cut out to secure her silence, but she weaves her story on a tapestry. When killed by the king she is transformed into a nightingale, whose lovely notes do contain a certain haunting melancholy.

The Song Thrush, like the nightingale in the Greek myth, is another glorious singer. The bird is omnivorous, but is particularly fond of snails, and will use an anvil, usually a stone, to break them open. The evidence can be seen scattered around in broken shells.

Song Thrush, *Turdus philomelos*.

Part of the spectacular high Andean railway that leads into Rock Earthcreeper habitat.

Upucerthia andaecola
Rock Earthcreeper

The genus name comes from the Latin word *upupa*, which means a 'hoopoe' or a 'pick-axe'. *Certhia* comes from the Greek word *kerthios*, which was used by Aristotle to describe a small bird.

The specific name comes from a geographical term, relating to the Andes, and the Latin word *colere*, meaning 'to dwell'. The long, decurved, 'hoopoe-like' bill is plunged into the ground to feed on arthropods, and the bird is almost totally terrestrial.

There is little chance of seeing this earthcreeper anywhere below an altitude of 2,800m (9,200ft).

A Birding High

This is indeed a high-altitude bird. The author boarded a train in Argentina called *Tren a Las Nubes* ('train to the clouds'). After disembarkment a walk leads to some flat ground at an elevation of more than 4,300m (14,100ft). Movement is done in stages, due to the high elevation and the concomitant altitude sickness, and all the birds look strange! A small café at the top provides a brew made with coca leaves, to relieve the nausea and headache in a location which is at the same altitude as the base camp at Everest.

Upupa epops
Common Hoopoe

The genus name is onomatopoeic and mimics the bird's song.

The specific name has a Greek origin. The first syllable, *epi*, means 'over' or 'above'. *Ops* is the Greek word for an 'eye'.

The word *epops* may have an 'overseeing' concept. The hoopoe is perhaps reminiscent of a guardsman with a crested helmet.

Hoopoe, *Upupa epops*.

A Bird with a Sinister Reputation

In the play *The Birds*, by the Greek playwright Aristophanes (c.446–386 BC), *Epops* is the main character. The bird was originally King Tereus, transformed into a Hoopoe by the gods as punishment for his crimes. The Hoopoe, it seems, had a bad reputation in antiquity. He was found in rocky barren places, among gravestones and sepulchres. This association with the sinister and occult is found in Aristotle, Pliny and other Greek writers. Hoopoe body parts were used as magical concoctions in antiquity.

At the nest, a number of anti-predatory devices are used. The nesting female produces foul-smelling liquid from the uropygial gland, which can be directed at an intruder or rubbed into her own plumage. The secretion smells like rotting meat. Young birds in the nest can direct their faeces at unwelcome visitors, and hiss at them like a snake. Perhaps *epops* does deserve its reputation, despite its great beauty.

Hoopoe, *Upupa epops*, with crest raised.

Vanellus armatus
Blacksmith Lapwing

See *V. vanellus* (below) for details of genus name.

Armatus is a Latin word which means 'armour', and refers to the spur on the carpal joint of the wing.

The English name refers to the metallic *tink-tink-tink* of the alarm call, which suggests a blacksmith's hammer striking an anvil. The species is widespread in Africa, and is very aggressive during the breeding season when it will fearlessly attack any intruder, including birds, animals and humans.

– V. gregarius
Sociable Lapwing

The species name comes from the Latin word *grex*, which means 'crowd'. See *V. vanellus* (below) for details of genus name.

The Sociable Lapwing was usually seen in small groups. Scientists reckoned the entire world population could be as low as 400 birds, until a huge flock (*grex*) of 3,200 was seen in Turkey in 2007. Even so, the species remains listed as Critically Endangered.

– V. vanellus
Northern Lapwing

The genus and species name comes from the Latin word *vannus*, which means a 'winnowing fan'. Reference is made to the wing-beats as the bird tumbles through the air.

Northern Lapwing, *Vanellus vanellus*. The name 'lapwing' refers to the bird's distraction display around the nest, when it drags a wing as if injured, to lure away predators.

Various local names mimic its call, including peewee, peewit, pewit, and so on.

In The Netherlands there is an annual competition to find the first lapwing egg, and each year seems to give an earlier date. The most recent holds the record – 3rd March – perhaps reflecting climate change, or perhaps do to the use of more efficient fertilisers to 'green' the nesting areas. The collection of lapwing eggs is now illegal, but they were considered a great delicacy in Victorian times.

Vermivora chrysoptera
Golden-winged Warbler

The genus name comes from two Latin words. *Vermis* is the word for a 'worm', and *vorare* is the verb 'to eat'.

The species name comes from two Greek words. *Chrysos* is the word for 'gold', and *pterux* is the word for 'wing'.

In 1989, a Golden-winged Warbler found its way across the Atlantic and settled in a supermarket car park in southeast England. As a 'special offer' – this was the first-ever sighting in the UK – the warbler drew in an estimated crowd of 3,000 birdwatchers.

In its North American breeding range there is much hybridisation with the closely related Blue-winged Warbler, which threatens the species' genetic purity.

Vestiaria coccinea
'I'iwi

The genus name comes from *vestitus*, the Latin word for 'clothing'.

The species name is based on the Latin word *coccinatus*, meaning 'clothed in scarlet'.

The alternative name for this species is Scarlet Honeycreeper.

As with the vanga family in Madagascar, a single honeycreeper ancestor has evolved to fill various ecological niches in Hawaii. The different species have a range of different bill-types, from thick finch-like bills to slender down-turned bills, each adapted to feed on a specific food, whether it be snails, insects, nectar, fruit or seeds.

These lovely birds are now highly endangered. Rats arrived in the 1800s, and now there is the threat from mosquitos carrying avian malaria, over which the honeycreepers have no resistance. To try to save these birds there are schemes to eradicate rats and other invasive species, and also to exterminate the mosquito population.

A Dying Breed?

El Jaguar, a cloud forest reserve in Nicaragua, used to be an important stop-off for Golden-winged Warblers as they passed south on migration through Mexico, Honduras, Guatemala, Costa Rica and Panama. The author visited the site in 2014, and that year just a single bird was seen at El Jaguar, instead of the hundreds that used to pass through.

Habitat in the bird's migration corridor has become degraded as trees are cut down to raise cattle and grow coffee. Without places to stop and feed, many birds die on the journey. Much effort has gone into persuading farmers to leave enough canopy trees for the birds to rest and feed, but it may be too late, and the warbler's future remains uncertain.

The *'I'iwi*, *Vestiaria coccinea*, showing off its bill, which is perfectly adapted for drinking nectar.

Vireo flavifrons
Yellow-throated Vireo

The genus name comes from the Latin verb *virere*, which means 'to be green'.

The species name comes from two Latin words. *Flavea* means 'yellow', and *frons* means 'front'.

This attractive songster breeds in eastern North America and winters south to northern South America.

– V. olivaceus
Red-eyed Vireo

The species name comes from the New Latin word *olivaceus*, which means 'olive-green'. *Oliva* is the Latin for 'olive'.

This is a small American songbird which holds the record for the most bursts of song sung in a single day. One single tireless singer clocked up a total of 20,000.

The vireo's nest is often parasitized by cowbirds. The word 'parasite' appears often in bird literature. *Parasitos* is a Greek word making reference to someone who eats at the table of another. This was an accepted lifestyle, and in exchange for food and lodging, the *parasitos* would provide entertainment, flattery, and a willingness to be humiliated.

Vultur gryphus
Andean Condor

The genus name comes from *vultur*, the Latin word for 'vulture', and the species name comes from the Greek word *grupos*, meaning 'hook-nosed'.

The word condor comes from *kuntur*, the Quechua word for 'condor'.

This is a huge bird with a wingspan of 3m (10.5ft). The middle toe is elongated and the rear toe is small, so the feet are adapted for walking. Wings are flapped when the bird rises from the ground, then the condor relies on thermals to stay aloft.

The Andean Condor frequently features in folklore and mythology. At the Yawar Fiesta in Peru, a condor is tied to the back of a bull. The bird pecks and claws the bull to death, to symbolise the power of the Andean people (the condor) over the Spanish (the bull).

Strange but beautiful – the Terek Sandpiper, *Xenus cinereus*.

Xenops rutilus
Streaked Xenops

The genus name comes from two Greek words. *Xenos* means 'strange', and *psao* comes from the verb 'to look'.

Rutilus is a Latin word meaning 'golden-red'. Literally, this South American species is a 'strange-looking golden-red bird'. In appearance it is somewhere between a tit and a nuthatch. The upper mandible is upturned, and used as a chisel to prise out insects and ants from decaying wood. The bird is often found in mixed-species feeding flocks, as flocking behaviour seems to reduce the danger of predation.

Xenus cinereus
Terek Sandpiper

The genus name comes from *xenos*, the Greek word for 'strange'.

Cinereus is Latin for ash-grey.

The English name makes reference to the Terek river, which flows into the Caspian Sea.

The bird feeds in a distinctive way, actively chasing insects and other mobile prey, and often running along the edge of the water to clean its catch.

A Terek Sandpiper trapped recently in Belarus bore a ring on its leg indicating that it was at least 17 years old. The bird therefore had 200,000km (125,000 miles) under its belt.

A singing White-throated Sparrow, *Zonotrichia albicollis*, showing off its splendidly striped head.

Zonotrichia albicollis
White-throated Sparrow

The genus name comes from two Greek words. *Zony* is the word for 'band', and *trichis* is the word for 'hair'.

The species name comes from two Latin words. *Albus* is the word for 'white', and *collum* is the word for 'neck'.

The bird's facial markings are so crisp and clear that they become a perfect lesson in anatomy. Nothing in the facial pattern is smudged: the yellow lores, black malar stripe, white crown, black eye-stripe and white throat all stand out clearly. The song is also a good identifier, rendered as 'Oh-sweet-Canada'.

The White-throated Sparrow is a rare transatlantic vagrant, and the 13th record for Britain was found by the author in Shetland. Dear reader, please excuse the lack of humility!

Zoonavena grandidieri
Madagascar Spinetail

The genus name comes from the Greek '*zoon*' which means an 'animal', and the Latin verb *navir*, 'to draw apart', referring to the spread out tail-spines.

The species name honours the French naturalist Alfred Grandidier (1836–1921). It was family wealth that enabled the young Grandidier brothers, Ernest and Alfred, then only in their early twenties, to begin a world tour in 1856, during

White's Thrush, *Zoothera aurea*, making a rare foray into the open.

which they amassed a huge collection of skins. Without the high quality medicines available today, periods of recuperation were necessary after various tropical ailments rendered them immobilised. Fever, for example, prevented an exploration of the Tibetan Plateau. Alfred's greatest interest was the avifauna of Madagascar, of which he wrote an exhaustive account. He also helped to map out the contours of the island.

This is a small forest swift, and is readily identified as the wings are held below the horizontal in level flight, while the spines which constitute the tail can be clearly seen. The species can also be found in the Comoro Islands.

Zoothera aurea
White's Thrush

The genus name comes from two Greek words. *Zoon* is the word for an 'animal', and *theras* is the word for a 'hunter'.

Aurea is a Latin word meaning 'golden'.

The English name makes reference to Gilbert White (1720–1793), a parson-naturalist who lived as a curate in the vicarage at Selbourne, Hampshire. White helped to shape the modern attitude of respect for nature, and wrote poetically about the humblest of creatures. To White the earthworm might look despicable, but without its presence the most basic processes of vegetation couldn't continue.

INDEX

Roman font = common name, *Italic* font = scientific name